Weather Contents

The Weather Around You. . . 2

What Makes Weather?. 4

The Water Cycle 11

Clouds 12

Weather Events 16

Watching the Weather. . . . 25

More About Weather 29

Weather Log 30

The Weather Around You

Step outside. Weather is all around. It is wind in your hair, sun on your skin, rain in your soggy shoes.

Lots of things you do depend on the weather. Should you ride your bike or curl up on the sofa and read? Should you wear shorts or long pants? Weather also affects how you feel. A rainy day might make you quiet and thoughtful. A sunny day might make you happy and excited.

Weather Write

Turn to the weather log on pages 30 and 31. As you use this book, record your daily weather observations on the log. To begin, write the name of the month at the top of the log. A sample entry is filled in for you.

2

What's the Weather Like?

Look at the pictures of different kinds of weather. Write words to describe each picture. Choose words from the box or think of other words.

hot	sunny	rainy
cool	damp	calm
freezing	breezy	drizzly
wet	dry	soggy
windy	still	humid
		chilly

_____

_____

_____

_____

_____

_____

What Makes Weather?

Heat from the sun, or **temperature**, and the push of the air on the earth, or **air pressure**, make weather happen. Weather also happens because of **wind** and wetness in the air, or **moisture**.

Weather Write

Read the temperature on a thermometer hanging in a shady place. Record the temperature on the weather log. Add to the log every day at about the same time.

Temperature

A **thermometer** measures temperature. The warmer the weather, the higher the liquid in a thermometer rises. Temperature is measured in degrees. These thermometers go up and down by two-degree steps from 0°.

This thermometer says 32°, the temperature at which water freezes.

This thermometer says 76°.

This thermometer says 56°.

What's the Temperature?

Read the thermometers. Write each temperature in the box. Then draw a line from each child to the temperature for which he or she is dressed.

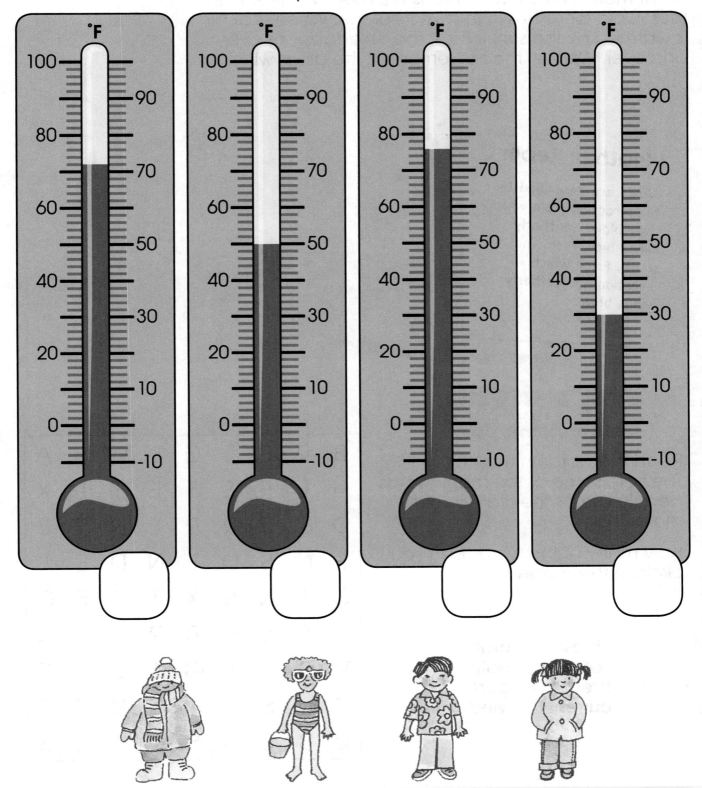

Wind

Wind is moving air. Some days are so still it seems that no air is moving at all. Don't be fooled, though. Air is always there, even when you don't notice it.

What makes wind? When air is warmed by the sun, it rises. Cold air rushes in to take its place. When that air is warmed by the sun, it rises, too. This happens over and over. We feel this movement of the air as wind.

Weather Report

Winds are described by the direction from which they blow. Southerly winds blow from the south. From which direction do northerly winds blow?

_____

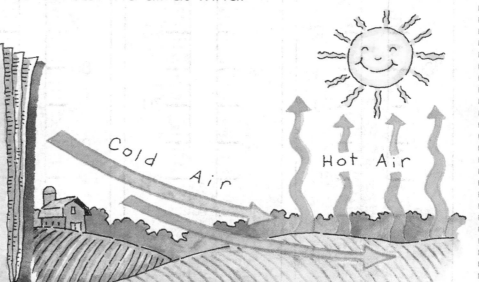

Cold Air

Hot Air

Airy Word Puzzle

Read the words in the box. They are some of the many words people use as they talk about moving air.

How many of the words can you circle in the puzzle?

blast	draft
blow	gale
breeze	gust
current	wind

B	R	E	E	Z	E	W	B	A
H	L	F	S	T	E	I	L	X
D	C	U	R	R	E	N	T	B
F	N	S	D	L	N	D	E	L
O	T	N	R	X	T	P	E	O
I	S	L	A	B	R	O	D	W
V	S	T	F	G	A	L	E	E
G	U	S	T	T	E	R	G	S
U	B	L	A	S	T	U	L	B

Moisture

Water is what makes Earth different from other planets. Water makes life possible. It also helps make Earth's weather.

When water in oceans, lakes, and rivers is heated by the sun, some of it **evaporates**, or turns into an invisible gas called **water vapor**.

The Case of the Missing Water

Try this experiment with evaporation.

You Need

- 2 clear measuring cups that are the same size

1. Fill both measuring cups about half full of water.

2. Place one uncovered measuring cup in a sunny, indoor spot and the other cup in a shady, indoor spot. From which measuring cup do you think the water will evaporate quicker?

_____

3. After a few days, check the cups. Has the water level changed? In what way? If not, wait a few more days. On the chart, record the amount of water in each cup.

	Water in Sun	Water in Shade
Day 3		
Day 5		
Day 7		

From which cup did the water evaporate quicker? _____

Why? _____

Water vapor rises and cools. Cool air can't hold as much water vapor as warm air can, so some of the vapor turns into tiny drops of water. This is called **condensation**.

Dew and frost are two kinds of condensation. After a warm, dry day, water from air near the ground condenses as it cools. Drops of water called **dew** form. You can see dew on grass, spiderwebs, and everything else close to the ground. In cold weather, when the temperature goes below freezing, or 32°F, dew changes to **frost**.

Word Watch

Precipitation is water in the form of rain, sleet, snow, or hail. Rain happens when the air is above freezing, or warmer than 32°. Sleet, snow, and hail happen when the air is below freezing.

Condensation on a Can

You Need

- a can of soda or juice

Put the can in the refrigerator. Leave it overnight. The next morning, take out the can and wait a minute or two. What do you see? Those drops are condensation. The can has cooled the air right next to it. You know that cold air can't hold as much water as warm air can, so the extra drops of water condense on the can.

Air Pressure

The weight of air pushing on the earth is called **air pressure**. Air pressure is another force that affects weather.

Air Pushes

You Need
- water
- a plastic or foam cup
- a postcard or index card

1. Fill the cup to the top with water.

2. Put the card over the top of the cup and hold it firmly.

3. Still holding the card, turn the cup upside down. Let go of the card. (Do this over a sink.)

What happens?

_____

_____

_____

The card stays under the cup because of air pressure. The air under the card pushes up so strongly it keeps the card in place, even though the water in the cup is pushing down.

Weather Puzzle

Write words from the box to complete the sentences.
Then fill in the puzzle.

Across

2. What we wear depends on the _____.

6. Rain, snow, and hail are kinds of _____.

7. Drops of water on a cold can are _____.

wind
water
air pressure
precipitation
condensation
weather
Evaporation

Down

1. _____ is what happens when water turns to water vapor.

3. The push of air on the earth is _____.

4. Cold air can't hold as much _____ as warm air can.

5. Moving air is _____.

The Water Cycle

Tiny drops of water gather together and make clouds. When clouds have more water than the air can hold up, the water falls to Earth as rain or snow.

Water Travels

The water on Earth travels on an endless **cycle**, or journey. There are three steps to the water cycle: evaporation, condensation, and precipitation. Write the steps where they belong in the picture.

_____

Water vapor makes a cloud.

_____

Rain and snow fall from clouds.

Word Watch

Meteorology is the science of weather. Weather scientists are called **meteorologists**.

_____

Heat from the sun changes water into water vapor.

Clouds

You've learned that clouds form when moist air rises and cools. Cool air can't hold as much water vapor as warm air. The water vapor starts to change into tiny drops of water or ice crystals that form clouds.

Watch out! Right now, I'm feeling like a cumulonimbus!

Cloud Shapes

Maybe you've looked at clouds in the sky and seen a dog, a tree, or some other shape. Look at the clouds in the picture. Circle the hidden shapes. How many can you find?

Different kinds of clouds bring different weather.

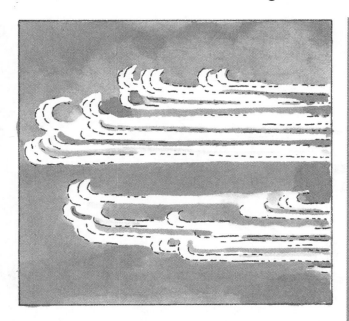

Cirrus clouds are thin, wispy streaks high in the sky. They are so high that the water inside them is ice.

Cumulonimbus clouds are large, gray thunderclouds. Thunderstorms, and even tornadoes, may come from these clouds.

Cumulus clouds look like big, puffy heaps or piles. They may start near the ground and rise into the sky like big towers.

Stratus clouds are thick, even layers low in the sky. They often make drizzling rain or snow.

Clouds are always changing. That's because the moisture at the edges of the clouds evaporates. Another reason clouds change is that the wind blows them.

Weather Write

Check the sky each day.
Do you see any clouds?
What kind are they?
Write the cloud names.

Cloudy Riddles

cumulonimbus
cirrus
stratus
cumulus

Write the cloud names to answer the riddles.

1. I look like a big, fluffy cotton puff. Who am I? _____

2. I'm dark and I can be noisy. People go inside when they see me.
   Who am I? _____

3. I'm light and feathery. Who am I? _____

4. I like to spread out. When I'm in a gray mood, I drizzle.
   Who am I? _____

Fantastic Cloud Maker

With a little help, you can make your own cloud.

You Need
- a clear glass jar
- plastic wrap
- ice
- hot tap water

1. Ask an adult to fill a jar with hot tap water and then pour out half the water.

2. Cover the jar with plastic wrap. Be careful not to burn your hands on the jar.

3. Place several ice cubes on top of the plastic wrap.

What do you see?

_____

_____

_____

Why did it happen?
(Turn back to page 11 for help.)

_____

_____

_____

Word Watch

Fog is a stratus cloud at ground level. Like a cloud, fog contains millions of tiny water drops. Fog forms when water vapor condenses near the ground.

Mist is like fog, except much thinner.

Smog happens when smoke and other kinds of dirt mix with fog.

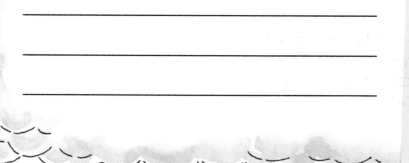

Weather Events

Rain and Rainbows

When the water inside a cloud becomes too heavy for the air to hold up, rain falls.

Make a Rain Gauge

You Need

• a measuring cup

Make a rain gauge to measure the amount of rain that falls where you live. Here's how.

Put a measuring cup outside where it will collect rainwater. Each week, record the amount of rain in the measuring cup in your weather log. Compare rainfall from week to week.

Rainbows are arcs of colors seen in the sky opposite the sun. They are caused by sunlight shining through small drops of water. Rainbows are made of red, orange, yellow, green, blue, indigo, and violet light. The colors in a rainbow are always in the same order.

Weather Report

Here's a way to remember the colors in a rainbow in the right order. Think of the name Roy G. Biv. Each letter stands for a color in the rainbow, starting with red at the top and ending with violet.

Your Own Rainbow

On a sunny day, you can make your own rainbow.

You Need
- a large glass of water
- a piece of white paper
- crayons or colored markers

Place the glass of water on a sunny, indoor windowsill. Put a piece of white paper on a table beside the windowsill. Slide the paper around on the table until colors appear on the paper. You've made a rainbow!

Color the rainbow below. Make sure the colors are in the right order.

Thunderstorms

Thunderstorms are caused by electricity that builds up in clouds. When the electricity is strong enough, a spark leaps from one cloud to another or to the ground. That spark is **lightning**. As lightning travels, the heated air around it expands so quickly that it explodes, making the loud noise we call **thunder**. Although thunder and lightning happen at the same time, you see lightning before you hear thunder because light travels much faster than sound.

How did the lightning leave the party?

In a flash.

You're Electric!

You Need

- a balloon

Electricity is around you all the time. There is even some in your body.

Try this simple experiment. Rub an air-filled balloon on your clothes. Press the balloon against a smooth wall. Static electricity will make the balloon cling. Rub the balloon again and see what happens when you touch it to your hair.

Snowstorms

Snow forms when ice crystals in a cloud bump into each other and stick together. If the air temperature below the cloud is cold enough, snow falls.

Weather Report

All snowflakes have six sides. Some snowflakes are made of as many as 100 ice crystals. No two snowflakes are alike.

Flake Detective

You Need

- black construction paper
- a magnifying glass
- colored pencils

On the next snowy day, put a piece of black construction paper in the refrigerator for a few minutes. Then take the paper outside and place it on the ground. Look through a magnifying glass at some of the snowflakes that land on the paper. (Don't breathe on the flakes! You'll melt them.) Draw what you see.

Blizzards

Blizzards are very bad snowstorms. They bring strong winds and lots of snow, either falling from the sky or being blown about by the gusty wind. Blizzards are dangerous because it's hard to see and temperatures are very low. Some blizzards are so severe that people in the country have gotten lost going from their house to their mailbox!

Homeward Bound

Find your way home through the snowstorm.
Watch out for snowbanks!

Tornadoes

Tornadoes are big whirlwinds of air that can swirl faster than 200 miles an hour. They may happen when a mass of cool, dry air runs into a mass of warm, damp air. The warm air rises quickly, thunderclouds form, and a twisting funnel of air begins to spin downward.

When tornadoes move on land, they can destroy everything they touch. Like huge vacuum cleaners, they suck up things in their paths.

Twister Fixer

A tornado has picked up things and dropped them in the wrong places. Circle the misplaced objects.

Tornadoes may not move at all, or they may travel as fast as 70 mph. They happen most often in the midwest and some southern parts of the United States in spring and early summer.

Weather Report

A **tornado watch** means that even though it may be sunny now, conditions are just right for the sort of thunderstorms that bring tornadoes. A **tornado warning** means that storms are happening, and a tornado has been spotted nearby. You should seek shelter now!

What are sleeping twisters?

Tornadoze.

Tornado Nicknames

The words in the box are some of the many names for tornadoes. How many can you find in the puzzle? Circle them.

cyclone
twister
funnel
whirlwind

spinner
vortex
churn

W	H	I	R	L	W	I	N	D
H	L	F	X	P	I	N	L	X
D	C	Y	C	L	O	N	E	T
F	U	N	N	E	L	D	V	W
O	T	N	R	C	T	P	O	I
F	N	S	D	H	J	G	R	S
V	S	T	B	U	N	L	T	T
G	P	S	T	R	K	R	E	E
S	P	I	N	N	E	R	X	R

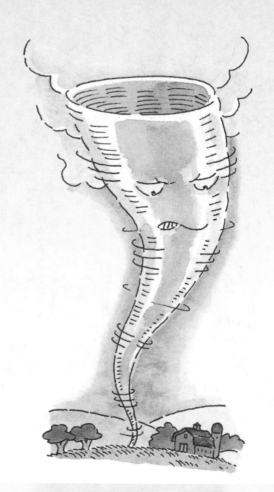

Hurricanes

Like tornadoes, **hurricanes** are powerful, whirling storms. Hurricanes are much larger than tornadoes, though. Hurricanes form over warm oceans and can travel hundreds of miles.

As the summer sun heats the sea, warm water vapor rises into the air and forms large thunderclouds. If there is wind, masses of clouds may begin to whirl strongly. As hurricanes move over the ocean, they create huge waves that can crash on shore. Hurricanes may move over land, bringing high winds and heavy rains.

Weather Report

To keep track of the hurricanes that happen each year, meteorologists name them. The first hurricane of the new year is given a name starting with the letter A. The next hurricane is given a name starting with B, and so on.

Get to the Eye!

The eye of a hurricane is the calm part at the center. Find your way through the hurricane to its eye.

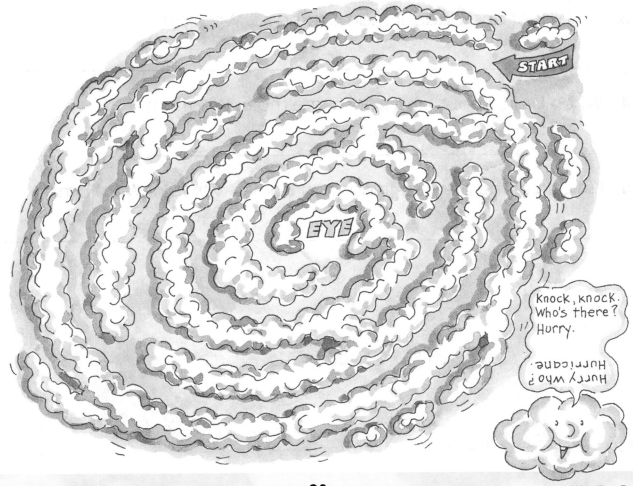

What Am I?

Write a word from the box after each clue.

tornado
thunderstorm
rainbow
hurricane
snowstorm

Weather Report

During hurricane season, watch the news for reports of hurricanes. Keep track of each hurricane's name and where the hurricane starts and ends.

1. My favorite dance is the twist. What am I?

_____

2. I turn everything white. What am I?

_____

3. I'm bigger and badder than a tornado. What am I?

_____

4. When I rain, I pour, and pour some more. What am I?

_____

5. I'm one of the prettiest things that comes with rain. What am I?

_____

Watching the Weather

Checking the weather is one of the first things many people do each day, especially people who work outdoors.

Outdoors in All Kinds of Weather

This puzzle includes some of the outdoor activities affected by the weather. Write words from the box to complete the puzzle.

Across

3. My crops need rain—but not too much!
4. Dry rocks make my sport easier.
5. I fly high to avoid storms.
7. I help you cross streets in all kinds of weather.
9. There can't be too much snow for me!
10. My white ball gets wet from dew on the grass.

Down

1. Neither rain nor snow keeps me from my route.
2. I cast my nets in calm or rough seas.
6. My truck goes slower in bad weather.
8. No matter what the weather, I tend my flowers.

mail carrier
farmer
skier
crossing guard
golfer
gardener
climber
fisherman
pilot
driver

Fact or Superstition

People have many beliefs about weather.
Some of them are true, but others are superstitions.

Fact: People use pinecones as weather
gauges. In dry weather, pinecones dry out
and open. When rain is coming, pinecones
absorb water in the air and close up.

Fact: Have you noticed that crickets chirp
louder in hot weather? When it's warm,
adding 37 to the number of chirps you
hear in 15 seconds will about equal the
temperature.

Superstition: Custom says that if a
groundhog comes out of its hole and sees
its shadow on February 2, winter weather
will last for six more weeks.

Superstition: Some people believe that woolly bear caterpillars' stripes can predict whether a winter will be mild or severe. They think that if the caterpillars' brown stripes are wider than the black stripes, winter will be mild. If the black stripes are wider, winter will be severe. Scientists say that the size of its stripes has to do with the age of a woolly bear caterpillar.

Superstition: Many people believe that birds go back to their nests before storms. Some people think the early or late migration of birds can predict whether winter will come early or late.

Fact or Superstition? Red sky at night, sailors' delight. Red sky at morning, sailors take warning.

This old saying means that a red sunset will be followed by good weather, and a red sunrise will bring storms. Watch the sunsets where you live. What do you notice?

_____

_____

_____

Find the Secret Words

waves
funnel
seven
thermometer
air pressure
meteorologists
cumulonimbus
blizzard

Answer the questions.
Then fill in the numbered boxes.

1. Four forces that make weather are heat,

   moisture, __ __ __ __ __ __ __ __ __ __ __ , and wind.
          6   10

2. We use a __ __ __ __ __ __ __ __ __ __ __ to measure
          9   2   7

   temperature.

3. Thunderstorms come from __ __ __ __ __ __ __ __ __ __ __ __
         3

   clouds.

4. Rainbows have __ __ __ __ __ colors.
        5

5. A very bad snowstorm is called a __ __ __ __ __ __ __ __.
              1

6. A tornado is a big whirlwind of air shaped like a __ __ __ __ __ __.
           11

7. Hurricanes make __ __ __ __ __ as they race over the ocean.
        8 12

8. Scientists called __ __ __ __ __ __ __ __ __ __ __ __ __
          4

   study weather.

Write the letters with numbers under them in the boxes
to describe yourself.

12	8	5	1	4	9	11	7	3	9	6	2	10

More About Weather

Information Books

Flash, Crash, Rumble, and Roll by Franklin M. Branley

Storms by Jenny Wood

Weather by Brian Cosgrove

Weather Forecasting by Gail Gibbons

Weather Words and What They Mean by Gail Gibbons

Video

The Unchained Goddess by Frank Capra

Storybooks

It Looked Like Spilt Milk by Charles G. Shaw

The Snowy Day by Ezra Jack Keats

Thunder Cake by Patricia Polacco

Weather Log

Month _____

Day	Temperature	Rainfall	Type of Weather
	89°	1/2"	
1			
2			
3			
4			
5			
6			
7			
8			
9			
10			
11			
12			
13			
14			
15			
16			

Types of Weather

rainy

snowy

foggy

cloudy

partly sunny

sunny

Day	Temperature	Rainfall	Type of Weather
17			
18			
19			
20			
21			
22			
23			
24			
25			
26			
27			
28			
29			
30			
31			

Look at the information on the weather log.

1. Has the weather gotten warmer or cooler during the month?

_____

2. How much rain fell?

_____

3. Which type of weather happened most often?

_____

Seeds and Plants Contents

What Is a Seed? 33

Look Inside a Seed 34

Seeds Come in All Shapes and Sizes 37

How Seeds Travel..41

What Do Seeds Need to Grow?..............45

From Seed to Plant......................................47

Plants Are Partners 51

All Kinds of Plants Grow from Seeds 53

How Fast Do Plants Grow? 54

How Plants Protect Themselves 55

Plants and Animals.....................................56

Plant Parts We Love to Eat 57

People Need Plants 58

What Is a Seed?

Have you ever seen a seed? Maybe you took a bite of a juicy, red apple and saw the small seeds inside. Perhaps you helped plant flower seeds or watched a squirrel gather acorns.

A seed is a package of plant life. Each seed has a little plant inside. Many seeds hold food, too.

Seeds are made by the male and female parts of flowers. Most seeds live inside fruit until they are ready to begin to grow into plants.

Plant Some Seeds

Plant sunflower seeds in the garden. Follow the arrow to plant the seeds.

Look Inside a Seed

You wear a coat to protect you from the cold. Seeds from flowering plants have **seed coats** to protect them. Inside the seed are one or two **food storage** parts. Next to the food storage parts is a baby plant, the **embryo** (**em**-bree-oh). The embryo has tiny leaves, a stem, and roots.

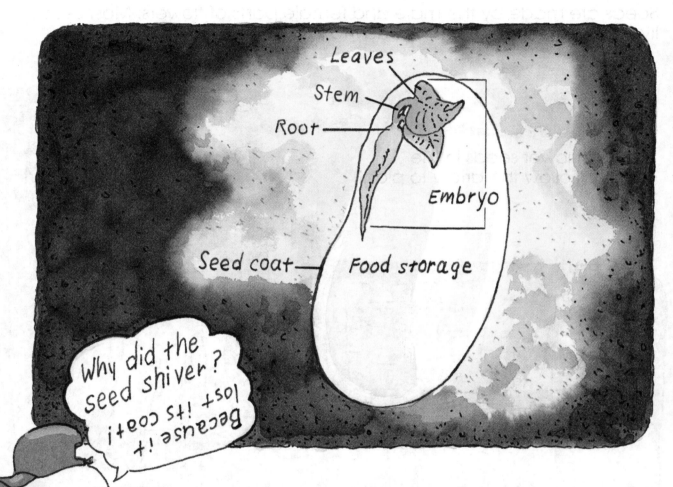

Why did the seed shiver? Because it lost its coat!

You wouldn't believe how many seeds plants make! But some seeds are eaten, and others fall in places where they can't grow. Some seeds freeze. Others get soaked and spoil. A few seeds, though, end up in places where they get the right temperature and enough air, water, and light to begin to grow, or **germinate** (**jur**-muh-nate).

Would you like to see the inside of a seed?
Let's look inside one kind of seed—a lima bean.

A Seed from the Outside In

You Need

- a dried lima bean
- a cup of water
- a magnifying glass

1. Fill a cup with water.

2. Put the lima bean in the water.

3. Leave the bean overnight.

4. Take the lima bean out of the water and look at it. Use a magnifying glass, if you have one.

What happened to the outside of the seed? Try to peel off the seed covering. Split the seed into halves. Look for the parts shown in the picture on page 34.

Draw the lima bean. Write the names of the parts of the seed where they belong.

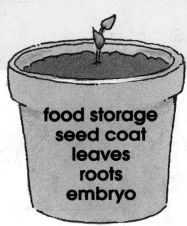

**food storage
seed coat
leaves
roots
embryo**

Seedy Word Puzzle

Write a word from the pot after each clue.
Then circle the words in the puzzle.

stem
water
plants
seeds
embryo

1. Seeds come from _____.

2. a baby plant inside a seed _____

3. one of the tiny parts inside the embryo _____

4. Seeds need _____ to grow.

5. Not all _____ grow into plants.

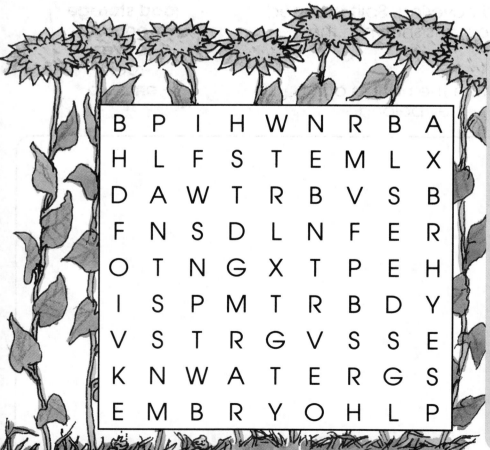

B	P	I	H	W	N	R	B	A
H	L	F	S	T	E	M	L	X
D	A	W	T	R	B	V	S	B
F	N	S	D	L	N	F	E	R
O	T	N	G	X	T	P	E	H
I	S	P	M	T	R	B	D	Y
V	S	T	R	G	V	S	S	E
K	N	W	A	T	E	R	G	S
E	M	B	R	Y	O	H	L	P

Most plants grow from seeds. But some can grow from other plant parts. Onions make parts that turn into **bulbs** and new plants. The bulbs are the part we eat.

Potato plants grow from **tubers**, thick parts of the stem that grow underground. Tubers can grow into plants. Tubers are the part we eat.

Seeds Come in All Shapes and Sizes

Just like people, seeds come in all shapes and sizes. Lima beans are fairly large seeds. Petunia seeds are so small you can hardly see them.

Many seeds have a cover, such as a fruit, a shell, or a pod. Can you think of any like this?

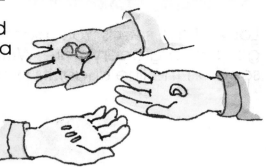

Acorn

Maple

Wild Carrot

Lettuce

Wild Rice

Poppy

Watermelon

An Ounce of Seeds

You Need
- a clear measuring cup
- a lot of sunflower seeds

1. Have an adult help you fill the measuring cup to the one ounce mark with sunflower seeds. How many seeds do you think are in one ounce?

_____

2. Pour out the seeds and count them. How many sunflower seeds are in one ounce?

_____

How close was your estimate?

_____

Name That Seed

Look at the seeds. You might find them in a yard, garden, or grocery store. Write the name of each seed on the line under its picture.

watermelon
coconut
corn

_____   _____   _____

1. Will the **largest** seed grow into the largest plant?
Take a guess. Check **yes** or **no**.

    ☐ **yes**   ☐ **no**

2. Will the **smallest** seed grow into the smallest plant?
Guess again. Check **yes** or **no**.

    ☐ **yes**   ☐ **no**

The milkweed seed is larger than the giant sequoia (suh-**kwoi**-uh) tree seed. But the milkweed plant grows to be only a few feet tall, while the sequoia tree can grow to be more than 300 feet high.

Look at the seeds and the plants into which they grow. Did you identify each kind of seed correctly? If not, look back at page 38 and write the correct names.

Compare the size of the seeds with the size of the plants. Small seeds can grow into large plants. Big seeds can become small plants. Seed size has nothing to do with the size of a plant.

Corn   **Coconut Palm**   **Watermelon**

Roasted Pumpkin Seeds

You Need

- pumpkin seeds
- a cookie sheet
- vegetable oil
- salt

1. Have an adult turn the oven to 250°.

2. Wash and dry some pumpkin seeds.

3. Pour a light coat of vegetable oil on a cookie sheet.

4. Spread the pumpkin seeds evenly over the sheet. Put salt on them, if you like.

5. Bake the seeds for about 15 minutes. Have the adult stir the seeds so they don't burn and return them to the oven for about 15 minutes more. When they turn golden brown, the seeds are done.

6. Cool the seeds. Share them with a friend.

You Need

- newspaper
- seeds of different sizes and shapes
- white glue
- cardboard or heavy paper

Make a Seed Picture

Put newspaper over your work area. Then set out your materials.

Cover the cardboard or heavy paper with glue. Arrange the seeds in a design you like. (Be sure to push the big seeds firmly into the glue.) Let your seed picture dry overnight.

It's in Code!

Fill in the missing code numbers. Then use the code to find the name of a large fruit that starts as a small seed.

a = 5	**b** =	**c** = 15
d =	**e** = 25	**f** = 30
g =	**h** = 40	**i** =
j =	**k** =	**l** = 60
m = 65	**n** =	**o** =
p =	**q** = 85	**r** =
s = 95	**t** = 100	**u** = 105
v =	**w** = 115	**x** =
y = 125	**z** = 130	

The largest seeds in the world come from the coco-de-mer tree. (**Coco-de-mer** means "nut of the sea.") One nut can weigh more than 50 pounds. That may be almost as much as you weigh.

80	105	65	80	55	45	70

How Seeds Travel

Imagine you live in a house with ten brothers and sisters. The family grows up, but no one moves out. You all get married and have children, still living in the same house together. Everyone is crowded!

Plants are like people that way. If they dropped their seeds right beside them, the seeds would be crowded too close together. Seeds have several ways to keep this from happening. One way is for animals to carry seeds to places where the seeds may have more room to grow.

Seeds Hitch a Ride

The seeds from these plants move from place to place by sticking to animal fur.

Spanish Needles

Use the code to figure out the missing words.

The seeds have ___ ___ ___ ___ ___ or
                     3   5   5   4   7

___ ___ ___ ___ ___ to help them cling.
2   1   6   2   7

Burdock

Code
1 = a
2 = b
3 = h
4 = k
5 = o
6 = r
7 = s

Seed Safari

You Need
- old white socks
- a big piece of white paper

Put the socks on over your shoes. Take a walk with an adult through a weedy, vacant lot, a field, or a park.

When you get home, take off the socks carefully. Shake them out over the paper. What do you see? Have any seeds stuck to the socks?

After they eat berries and other fruit, birds drop some of the seeds as they fly. This is another way that seeds are moved from place to place. Some seeds birds scatter are thistle seeds, apple seeds, and mistletoe seeds.

Drop a Berry in the Meadow

Help the cardinal find its way to the meadow, where it will drop the berry and scatter the seeds inside.

Do you ever forget things? Squirrels do! Sometimes, squirrels bury acorns and forget where they are. Some of the acorns grow into oak trees. Being buried by animals is another way seeds move.

Find the Acorns

Help the squirrel find the acorns it buried. Circle ten hidden acorns.

The wind moves some seeds from place to place. Have you ever blown on the soft, white seeds of a dandelion? Did the seeds fly through the air? Your breath was like a puff of wind.

Dandelion seeds aren't the only kind moved by wind.

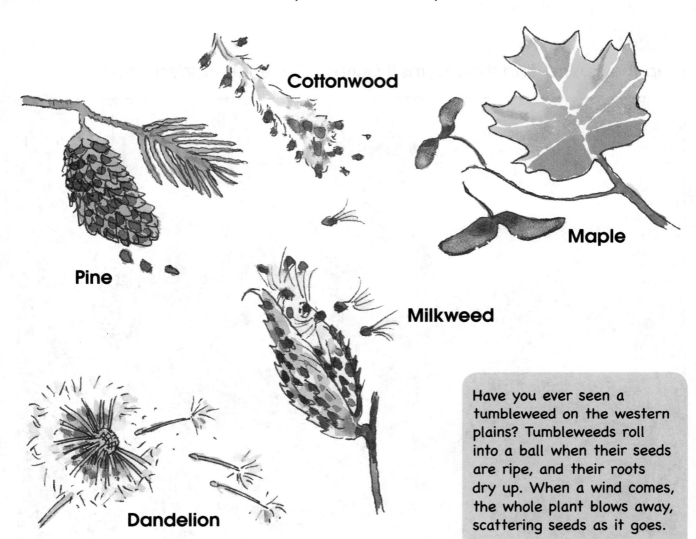

Pine

Cottonwood

Maple

Milkweed

Dandelion

Have you ever seen a tumbleweed on the western plains? Tumbleweeds roll into a ball when their seeds are ripe, and their roots dry up. When a wind comes, the whole plant blows away, scattering seeds as it goes.

Some plants drop their seeds near water. The water carries the seeds—sometimes to places where they can grow. Pussy willow seeds can be moved by water. Coconut seeds can fall into the ocean and grow into new plants if they reach land again.

WRITE NOW!
Splash! You're a coconut that has just fallen from a palm tree into the ocean. Take out a sheet of paper, and write what happens to you.

What Do Seeds Need to Grow?

Some seeds can wait a long time for everything to be just right so they can grow. If you look at a seed while it is waiting, you might see its wrinkled coat. The seed is not dead. It is just resting.

People need food to live and grow. Seeds do, too. Seeds need air, plenty of water, and the right temperature to germinate. Some seeds also need light.

You Need

- water
- paper towel
- a glass or plastic jar
- lima bean seeds from a seed package

Sprout a Seed

1. Wrap wet paper towels around the inside of a jar.

2. Have an adult help you fill the jar about one-fourth full with water.

3. Put a few lima beans between the inside of the jar and the paper towels.

4. Leave the jar on a windowsill in your house for about a week. Check each day to make sure the paper towels stay wet.

Your lima beans have germinated! They swelled up with water and broke through the seed coat. Lima beans are growing. The part growing up is the shoot. The part growing down is the root. Draw one of the seeds. Write **shoot** and **root** next to those parts.

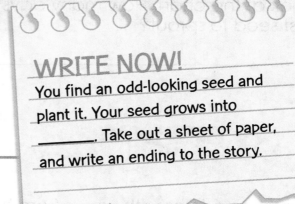

WRITE NOW!

You find an odd-looking seed and plant it. Your seed grows into _____. Take out a sheet of paper, and write an ending to the story.

Secret Seeds

Some seeds are so small it's hard to see them. Here's a way to watch for shoots from seeds you can't see.

You Need

- an empty milk carton
- soil from a yard or garden
- water

1. Have an adult cut the milk carton in half.

2. Fill the bottom half with soil.

3. Move the carton to a shady place inside the house. Circle the day of the week on the chart.

4. Water the soil daily to keep it moist.

5. Put a check mark on the chart by the day you see the first shoots.

	Sunday	Monday	Tuesday	Wedneday	Thursday	Friday	Saturday
Week 1							
Week 2							

Look at the chart. How many days did it take for the first seed to sprout?

_____

Seed Riddles

coat
leaves
germinate
roots
stem

Solve the riddles with words from the pot.

1. A seed doesn't have a hat, but it does have a _____.

2. A seed has no flowers, but it does have a _____, _____, and _____.

3. A seed doesn't have germs, but it does _____.

From Seed to Plant

This is how a new plant grows from a seed.

- The seed swells with water and bursts through its seed coat, or germinates.
- The roots grow down into the soil.
- The shoot grows up toward the sunlight.
- Leaves grow from the shoot.
- The plant gets bigger each day.
- Buds appear on the plant.
- Blossoms appear on the plant.

The plant is fully grown. It will have fruit with seeds inside. After a while, the fruit will ripen and the seeds will spill out. Some of the seeds will germinate and more plants will grow.

Sunflowers need so much sunlight they turn their heads during the day to face the sun.

Shoot

Seed

Root

Leaf

Bud

Blossom

Write the Parts

Write the names of the plant parts on the lines.

_____

_____

_____

The study of plants is called **botany**. A scientist who studies plants is a **botanist**.

What's That Sound?

You Need
- a cup of popcorn
- water
- a baking pan

Fill a cup nearly to the top with popcorn kernels. Add water to fill the cup completely. Then put the cup in a baking pan. Wait five or six hours. You'll hear some surprising sounds! What might the sounds be?

A Plant Grows Up

What's wrong with these pictures? A flowering plant is growing, but the order is all mixed up. Number the pictures from 1 to 6 in the correct order.

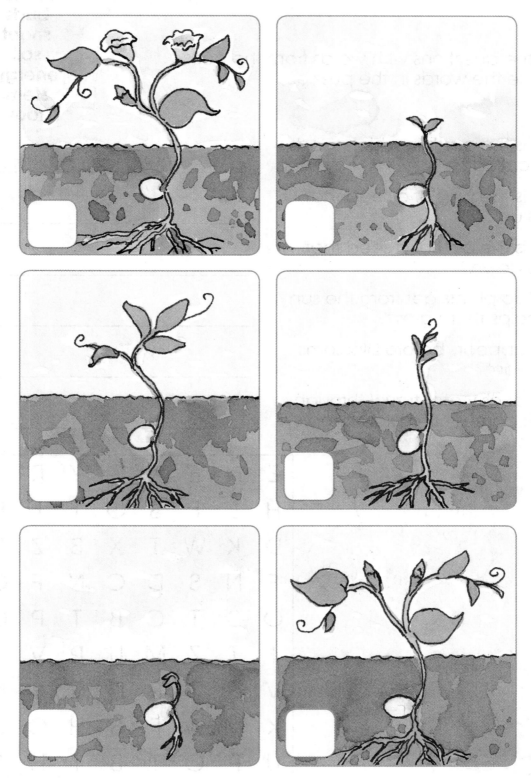

Plant Words

Answer the questions with words from the pot.
Then circle the words in the puzzle.

buds
shoot
soil
energy
stem
root

1. What is the earth in which seeds grow called? _____

2. What is the part of a seed that grows up? _____

3. What is the part of a seed that grows down? _____

4. What do plants get from the sun that helps them grow? _____

5. What appears before blossoms on a plant? _____

6. What does water travel through after it comes up a plant's roots? _____

What's the saddest seed?

A weeping willow!

E	N	E	R	G	Y	R	B	A
H	L	F	S	O	I	L	H	X
D	K	W	T	X	B	Z	R	B
F	N	S	D	C	N	F	O	R
O	S	T	C	B	T	P	O	H
I	T	Z	M	U	R	V	T	Y
V	E	T	R	D	V	S	N	E
K	M	W	F	S	H	O	O	T
U	P	O	T	B	I	H	L	P

Plants Are Partners

Plants take in air through tiny holes in their leaves. Plants take in water through the roots, up the stem, and into the leaves. Sunlight makes the air and water join to create the energy plants need to grow. New plants turn their leaves toward the light. They want to get as much energy as they can!

Animals and plants are partners. Here's how. Take a big breath of air. You just took in a gas called **oxygen**. Some of that oxygen comes from plants. Now breathe out. You just put a gas called **carbon dioxide** into the air. Plants use the carbon dioxide to make their food.

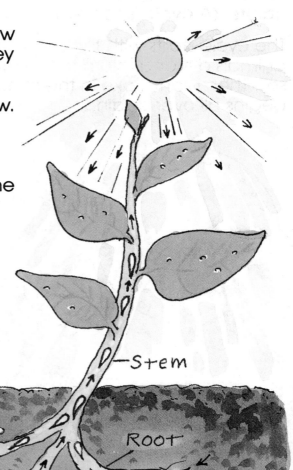

—Stem

Root

See Water Travel

You Need

- food coloring
- stalks of celery with leaves
- a glass of water

1. Ask an adult to put a few drops of red or blue food coloring in a glass of water. Place a stalk of celery with leaves into the glass, leaf end up.

2. Wait a few hours. What happened to the celery? Ask the adult to slice the celery the short way. Look at the colored paths in the celery that carry water.

You know that plants grow by taking energy from the sun, carbon dioxide from the air, and water from the ground. They give us food to eat and oxygen to breathe. This partnership is called the **cycle of nature**. (A **cycle** is something that is repeated.)

The cycle starts with the sun's energy. It ends when plants and animals die and return to the ground. There, they add minerals to the soil. Then plants take in the minerals with water from the soil. The cycle begins all over again.

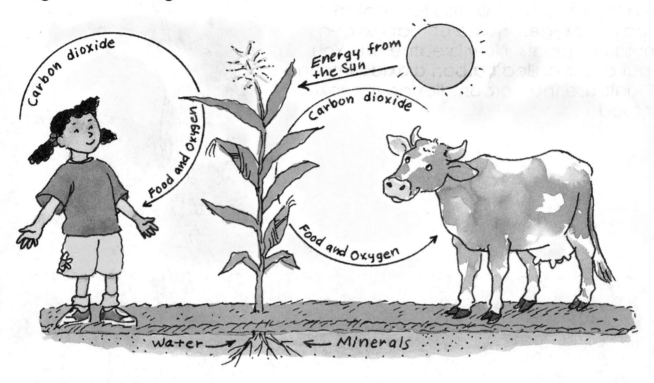

Cycle of Nature

1. What do plants get from the air? _____

2. How does it get into the air? _____

3. What do animals get from the air? _____

4. How does it get into the air? _____

All Kinds of Plants Grow from Seeds

Some seeds grow into plants with flowers that make gardens beautiful and sweet smelling. Some seeds become trees and bushes that shade people and give wood. Some seeds grow into plants that give tasty fruits and vegetables.

What's Growing?

The seeds in these pots are growing into plants. But what kind of plants are they? Read the clues. Then write the name of each plant under its pot.

corn
lily
bean
tomato

1. The name of this plant rhymes with **potato**.

_____

2. The name of this plant rhymes with **mean**.

_____

3. The name of this plant rhymes with **horn**.

_____

4. The name of this plant rhymes with **silly**.

_____

How Fast Do Plants Grow?

Here's another way plants are like people. Some grow slowly; others grow quickly. This year, you might have been like many trees, growing slowly and steadily. Or maybe you grew quickly, as a radish plant does.

How Much Did It Grow?

One kind of plant, **bamboo**, can grow as many as three feet in one day!

These four plants have been growing for three weeks.
How much did they grow?
Read the graph. Then answer the questions.

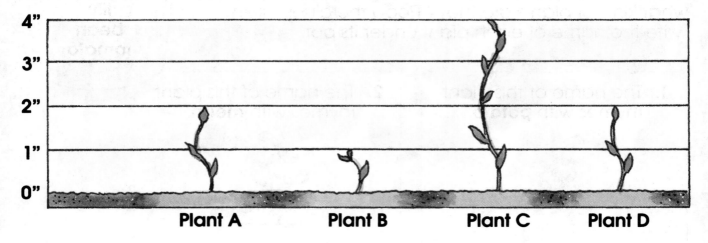

1. Which plant grew the most?

   _____

   _____

2. How much taller is the biggest plant than the smallest one?

   _____

   _____

3. Which two plants grew the same amount?

   _____

   _____

How Plants Protect Themselves

Some plants protect themselves from insects and other animals that would like to eat them. Spines, thorns, and prickles keep away large animals. Coatings of wax or stiff hairs on leaves keep away smaller ones. And what insect would want to eat leaves that taste terrible, such as those of citrus plants, or are poisonous, such as those of nightshade or foxglove?

Rose

Cactus

Poison Ivy

Another way that plants protect themselves is through **camouflage** (**kam**-uh-flazh), coverings or colors that make plants blend with their surroundings.

A Plant Fights Back

Think of a way a plant might protect itself. Draw your plant here.

Some plants don't have to worry about being eaten by animals. They eat animals instead. One of those plants, the Venus flytrap, has leaves that snap shut when an insect lands on them. The leaves open up again after the insect has been eaten.

Plants and Animals

Plants and animals help each other in different ways.

Helpers, Inc.

Read the clues. Write words from the pot that fit the shapes.

food
bury
drop
hide
carry
seeds

1. Many animals need plants for ⬜⬜⬜⬜.

2. Many animals eat ⬜⬜⬜⬜⬜.

3. Animals use plants to ⬜⬜⬜⬜.

4. Squirrels ⬜⬜⬜⬜ nuts.

5. Animals ⬜⬜⬜⬜⬜ seeds on their fur.

6. Birds ⬜⬜⬜⬜ seeds as they fly.

Plant Parts We Love to Eat

People and animals eat the fruits of some plants, the seeds of some, and the leaves and roots of others.

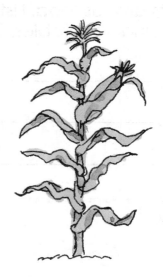

Do you recognize these plants? The one on the left is a sweet potato. What part do we eat? The one on the right is corn. What part of the corn plant do we eat?

1. _____

2. _____

These are different kinds of lettuce. What part of the plant do we eat?

3. _____

People Need Plants

There are more than 350,000 different kinds of plants!

Plants give us food. List some fruits and vegetables, and foods made from fruits and vegetables, that we eat.

_____

_____

_____

Plants are made into fiber for clothing.
What other kinds of clothes could be made from fiber?

_____

_____

_____

Trees are plants that give us wood for buildings and for fuel. Paper comes from trees, too. Can you think of anything else people use that comes from trees?

_____

_____

Many animals, including cows, pigs, and chickens, eat plants. Then cows give us milk, pigs provide meat, and chickens lay eggs. Write the names of other animals that eat plants.

_____

_____

Some plants make problems for people. Weeds can crowd out flowers in a garden or crops in a field. Some plants cause sneezes and itchy eyes. Others, such as poison ivy, bother the skin.

But plants help far more than they hurt. They keep the soil from blowing away. They slow down rushing water by holding some of it in their roots and stems. They are food for animals. The whole world needs plants. And most plants start with seeds.

The Truth About Seeds and Plants

You know a lot about seeds and plants! Take this quiz. Write **true** if the sentence is true. Write **false** if the sentence is not true. If you don't remember, look on the page or pages listed after the sentence.

1. Most seeds live inside fruit until they are ready to begin to grow. (p. 33) _____

2. The embryo of a seed has tiny fruits inside. (p. 34) _____

3. All seeds germinate. (p. 34) _____

4. All seeds are the same shape and size. (p. 37) _____

5. One way seeds travel is by sticking to animal fur. (p. 41) _____

6. Shoots grow down into the soil, and roots grow up toward the sun. (p. 45) _____

7. Buds appear before blossoms on a plant. (p. 47) _____

8. Plants need energy to grow. (p. 51) _____

9. Plants have thorns to attract insects. (p. 55) _____

10. People need plants to live. (p. 58-60) _____

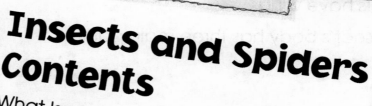

Insects and Spiders Contents

What Is an Insect?......................
Where Insects Live............................ 62
How Insects Grow.............................. 66
Insects That Live in Groups................. 68
How Insects Protect Themselves........ 72
Where Insects Go in Winter.............. 74
Insects and People 76
What Is a Spider? 78
Spiderwebs and Silk....................... 80
Kinds of Spiders............................. 82
What Spiders Eat 84
Spiders and People......................... 86
More About Insects and Spiders........ 88
.... 90

What Is an Insect?

Like you, insects are alive. Both people and insects are animals. But insects don't have bones inside their bodies as you do. Instead, they have a hard outer shell. Insects are different from other animals because they have six legs. Most adult insects have wings.

An insect's body has three main parts.

The **abdomen** is the "tail" end of the insect. Inside are the heart and breathing tubes. Some insects, such as bees, have a stinger on the end of the abdomen.

The **head** has eyes, antennae (an-**ten**-ee), and the parts that eat.

The **thorax** is right behind the head. The wings and legs are connected to the thorax.

WRITE NOW!

Yikes! Some kid just put you in a jar for an hour. What was it like? Take out a sheet of paper and write.

Ladybug, ladybird, lady beetle— whatever you call me, I'm an insect.

What's That Part?

Write the name of the part under each insect.

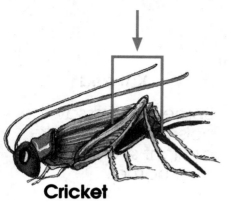

Cricket

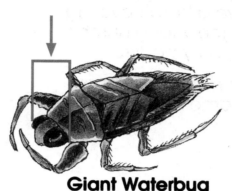

Giant Waterbug

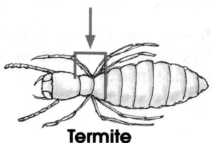

Termite

_____   _____   _____

Invent an Insect

Imagine that you discover a new kind of insect. Draw your discovery. Make sure your insect has three main body parts, six legs, and two antennae.

Make a Bug Catcher

To make a bug catcher, ask an adult to cut the top from a clear plastic bottle. Make a screen by cutting a slit in a piece of fabric. Attach it over the opening with a rubber band. Then go on a bug hunt. When you find an interesting bug, put it in the bottle.

Take your bug catcher into the shade. Look at the bug carefully. Is it an insect? Write notes or draw pictures. Keep the bug no longer than an hour. Bugs need to find their own food, water, and shelter.

* Children should not capture bees, wasps, or other stinging insects.

Insect Count

Not all crawlers and wrigglers are insects. Some tiny creatures have a hard covering and legs with joints, but the wrong number of legs. Some have soft, slimy bodies.

Take a close look at each animal. Count the legs. Then write its name under **Insects** or **Not Insects**.

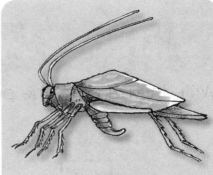

Katydid

Some people say the noise katydids make at night sounds like their name.

Millipede

Some millipedes give off a big stink if they are frightened.

Pill Bug

Pill bugs roll up in a tight ball when disturbed. Can you guess how they got their name?

Slug

Slugs leave a slimy trail when they move about.

Butterfly

The spots on the wings of this butterfly look like eyes and confuse the butterfly's enemies.

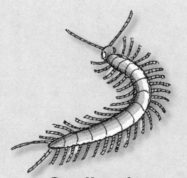

Centipede

Centipedes live under rotting logs and in other damp places.

Earthworm

Earthworms dig burrows in soil. They come out at night.

Dog Tick

Ticks suck the blood of dogs, cows, horses, and humans.

Tarantula

Some people think these fuzzy creatures make gentle pets.

Dragonfly

Dragonflies catch mosquitoes and eat them.

Insects	Not Insects

Awesome!

Insects don't have voices. But many insects make noises by rubbing parts of their body together. Have you heard a cricket's song? The cricket rubs its front wings together to make a cheerful sound.

What do you call a rabbit owned by a beetle?

A bug's bunny.

Where Insects Live

Insects live on dry land just about everywhere. In really cold places, such as the North Pole, they live in the fur of polar bears and other big, warm animals. In hot places, rainforests for example, insects are everywhere you look.

A few kinds of insects, but not too many, live in oceans. Quite a few kinds live in streams and ponds.

Watery Homes

Some kinds of insects live on or in water. Here are four of them.

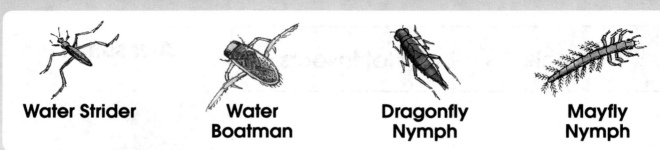

Water Strider **Water Boatman** **Dragonfly Nymph** **Mayfly Nymph**

Look at the underwater scene. Circle water striders in red and water boatmen in green. Draw blue circles around dragonfly nymphs and brown circles around mayfly nymphs. Then count each kind of water insect. Write the number of each kind.

Water Striders	Water Boatmen	Dragonfly Nymphs	Mayfly Nymphs
☐	☐	☐	☐

66

Insects All Around Us

The picture shows lots of insects in places where they often live. Do you recognize any of these insects? Make a list of the ones you know.

Awesome!
Don't look for a cricket's ears on its head. Its ears are on its legs!

Insects I Know

_____

_____

_____

_____

_____

_____

_____

monarch
walking stick
grasshopper
praying mantis
ant
bee
ladybug

Roll logs and rocks back where you find them. Then insects' homes are not destroyed.

How Insects Grow

Their hard outer skin helps insects. It's waterproof like a raincoat and protects like armor. The only problem is that insects' skin can't stretch. So, how do baby insects get bigger?

Insects get bigger when they climb out of the outside layer of their skin. After they slowly step out, the inner layer of their skin is soft and wet. It takes a while to dry and harden. While the insects wait, they can't run or fly away from enemies.

A Chinch Bug Grows Up

Have you ever seen this insect? It's a chinch bug. A young chinch bug looks like a small adult, except it has no wings.

Look at these pictures of a chinch bug. The youngest chinch bug is an egg. Each time the baby chinch bug shed its skin, it grew a little. Look at the ruler under each chinch bug. Number the chinch bugs in order from youngest to oldest. Write the numbers **1** through **5** under the correct pictures.

What Do You Say?

Every time an insect crawls out of its skin, it is growing up. Insects can't talk, but it's fun to pretend they can. Fill in the balloons to tell what they might say.

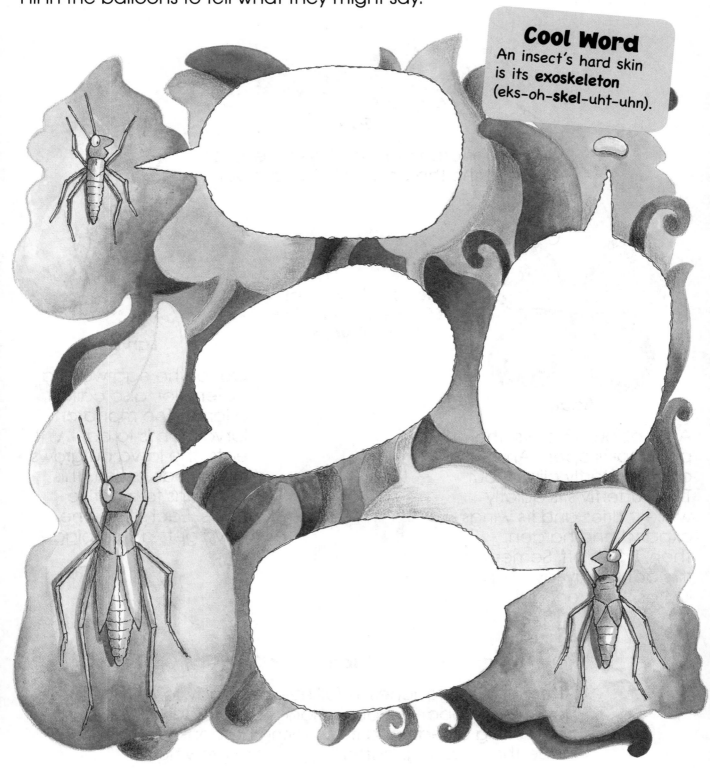

Cool Word
An insect's hard skin is its **exoskeleton** (eks-oh-**skel**-uht-uhn).

How Insects Grow

All insects start life as tiny eggs. The babies of some insects look totally different from their mothers and fathers. After some amazing changes, the babies grow up to look just like their parents.

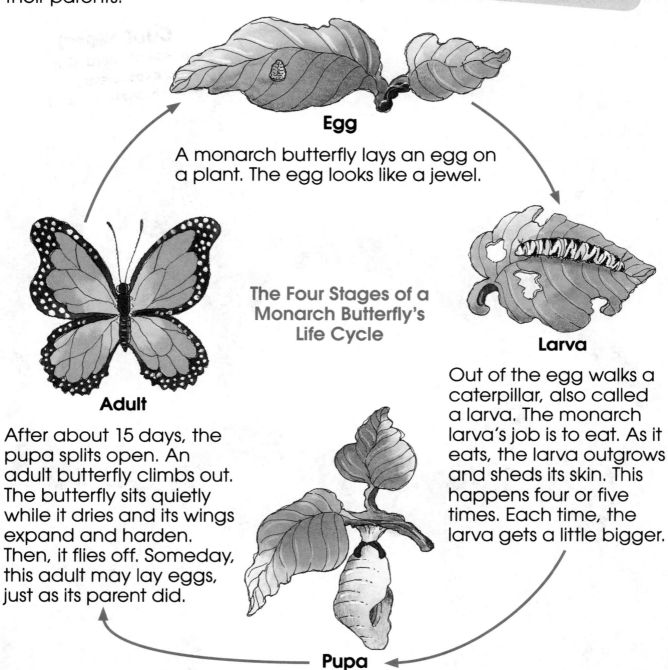

Egg

A monarch butterfly lays an egg on a plant. The egg looks like a jewel.

The Four Stages of a Monarch Butterfly's Life Cycle

Larva

Out of the egg walks a caterpillar, also called a larva. The monarch larva's job is to eat. As it eats, the larva outgrows and sheds its skin. This happens four or five times. Each time, the larva gets a little bigger.

Adult

After about 15 days, the pupa splits open. An adult butterfly climbs out. The butterfly sits quietly while it dries and its wings expand and harden. Then, it flies off. Someday, this adult may lay eggs, just as its parent did.

Pupa

After the larva reaches its full size, it is ready to become a pupa. The pupa hangs upside down from a twig or leaf, and its covering hardens. Inside the covering, butterfly parts are growing.

Monarch Word Search

Fill in the blanks with the words from the box.
Then circle the words in the puzzle.

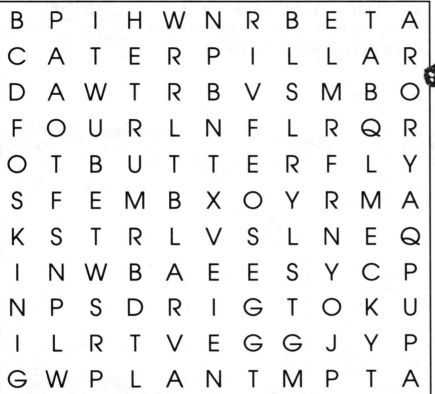

B	P	I	H	W	N	R	B	E	T	A
C	A	T	E	R	P	I	L	L	A	R
D	A	W	T	R	B	V	S	M	B	O
F	O	U	R	L	N	F	L	R	Q	R
O	T	B	U	T	T	E	R	F	L	Y
S	F	E	M	B	X	O	Y	R	M	A
K	S	T	R	L	V	S	L	N	E	Q
I	N	W	B	A	E	E	S	Y	C	P
N	P	S	D	R	I	G	T	O	K	U
I	L	R	T	V	E	G	G	J	Y	P
G	W	P	L	A	N	T	M	P	T	A

butterfly
four
larva
plant
caterpillar
pupa
egg
skin

1. An insect begins its life as an _____.

2. The monarch butterfly lays its egg on a _____.

3. The _____ comes out of the egg.

4. The larva is also called a _____.

5. The monarch sheds its _____ during the larva stage.

6. During the pupa stage, a _____ is forming.

7. The butterfly comes out of the _____.

8. The life cycle of a butterfly has _____ stages.

Insects That Live in Groups

Some kinds of insects live alone. Others live in big groups. Ants, bees, and wasps live in groups. An ant group is called a **colony**. The adult ants in the colony have different jobs. They work together to keep the colony alive.

Most ants dig an underground nest. It has tunnels and rooms. Some rooms are for the young larvae. Other rooms are for the pupa stage. Workers have sleeping rooms.

Why do bees hum? They forget the words!

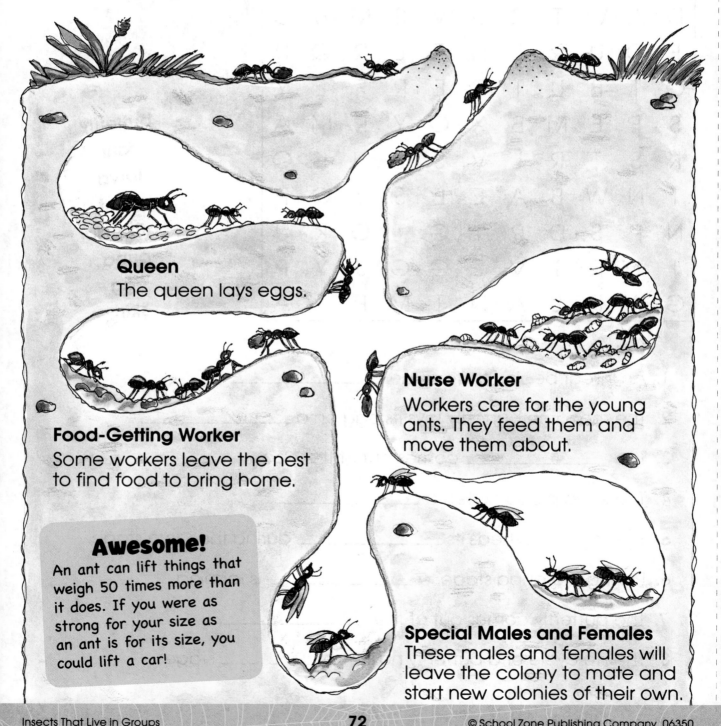

Queen
The queen lays eggs.

Nurse Worker
Workers care for the young ants. They feed them and move them about.

Food-Getting Worker
Some workers leave the nest to find food to bring home.

Awesome!
An ant can lift things that weigh 50 times more than it does. If you were as strong for your size as an ant is for its size, you could lift a car!

Special Males and Females
These males and females will leave the colony to mate and start new colonies of their own.

Have an Ant Picnic

One way to watch ants is to have a picnic. In this picnic, the treats are for the ants. Which foods will make the ants come running?

You will need small samples of foods. Foods you might choose include fruit, cereal, cooked meat, cookies, honey, crackers, and lettuce.

1. List the foods you picked for your ant picnic in the chart below. Predict the food or foods the ants will choose first.

2. Put a small piece of each food on its own paper plate.

3. Find a little hill of dirt that shows where an ant colony is. Put the plates in a circle around the anthill.

4. Wait and watch. On the chart, write an **X** in the **1** column for the food the ants find first. Write an **X** in the **2** column for the food the ants eat second. Do the same for the rest of the food.

Was your prediction correct? _____

Foods	1	2	3	4	5

WRITE NOW!

Be an ant or a bee with a BIG problem! You want to live all by yourself, not in a colony or hive. What will you do? Take out a sheet of paper and write.

* Some kinds of ants bite. Have your child wear shoes, socks, and long pants tucked inside the socks.

How Insects Protect Themselves

Bats eat insects. So do frogs, foxes, and birds. Many insects eat other kinds of insects. How do insects stay alive when so many creatures want to eat them?

Some insects protect themselves by stinging and biting. Wasps can give a painful sting. Insects that taste bad or sting have bright colors and patterns. This warns other animals to stay away, or else!

Some insects taste bad. A bird may try to eat a monarch butterfly once. But the monarch tastes so terrible it will never try to eat one again!

Keep away!
I taste terrible

Cool Word
Colors or shapes that hide an animal are **camouflage** (**kam**-uh-flazh).

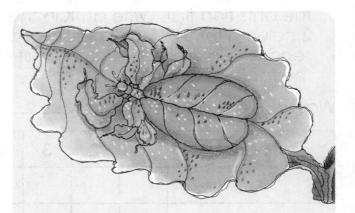

Hiding keeps other insects safe. Their small size helps them hide. Having colors and shapes that blend with their hiding places helps, too.

Hide-and-Seek!

A walking stick that isn't walking is hard to find. This insect's shape and color make it look just like the twigs on which it sits. Find the walking sticks. Circle each one. How many can you find?

Number of walking sticks: _____

Make a Showoff Butterfly

Make a butterfly with warning colors on its wings.

1. Fold a piece of paper in half. Then draw a butterfly's body on

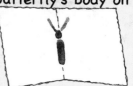

2. Put drops of paint on one side of the fold in the shape of a wing. Make a colorful design inside the wir

3. Press the two sides together. Open slowly to see two wings with warning colors.

Where Insects Go in Winter

You can find insects in winter if you look carefully. Black dots moving on snow on a warm winter day are insects called snow fleas.

Most adult female insects die before winter comes. Before she dies, a praying mantis may make 15 egg cases. She makes a foam nest on a plant stem. Then she lays her eggs inside the foam. The foam dries and hardens. In spring, the eggs hatch and the babies climb out.

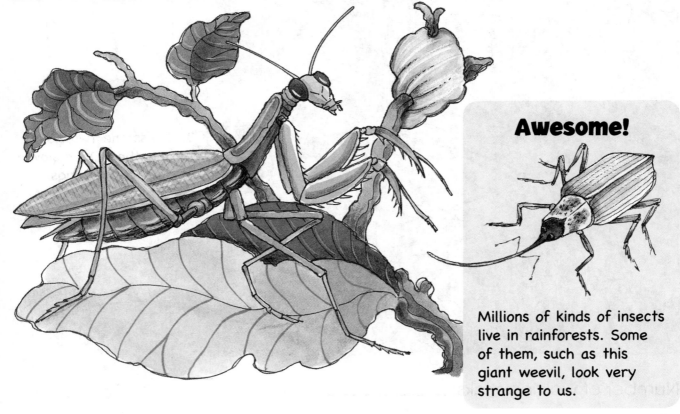

Awesome!

Millions of kinds of insects live in rainforests. Some of them, such as this giant weevil, look very strange to us.

Which Way Do I Go?

Some insects **migrate**, traveling to places with warm weather. Monarch butterflies are the world's most amazing insect travelers. Some monarchs that live in western North America spend the winter in sunny California. Monarchs in eastern North America fly south to warmer weather in Mexico.

If you live in the United States (except Hawaii and Alaska), find your state on this map. If it is a pink state, your monarchs may fly to California this fall. If you live in a green state, your monarchs will fly to Mexico for the winter. Draw a line to connect your butterflies' summer homes and winter homes.

Awesome!

If the burying beetle finds a dead mouse, the beetle buries it in the soil. Then the beetle lays its eggs nearby. When the eggs hatch, the baby beetles eat the mouse.

I fly up into the mountains for the winter. There I join hundreds of other ladybugs in a cave.

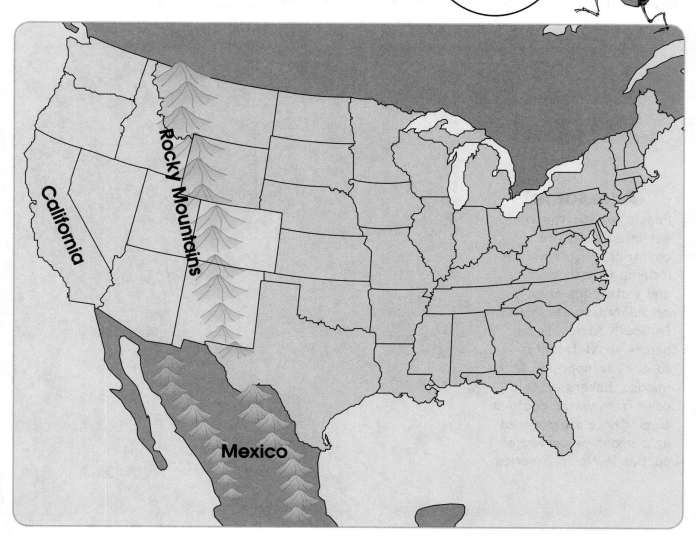

Insects and People

Do insects bug you? Mosquito bites itch. Ants and cockroaches get into food. Fleas bite our pets and sometimes us. Other insects eat farmers' crops as the fruits and vegetables grow.

Insects do plenty of good things, though. Many plants can't live without insects. Without bees, we'd have no apples or honey to eat. Insects are food for birds and other animals. Ants and beetles help get rid of dead plants and animals on the ground.

What bug likes picnics, wears a red suit, and has a long white beard?

Ant-a-Claus!

Insect Count

How many insects can you find in this picture? _____

Awesome!

People around the world eat insects. In Arab countries, people munch locusts. Grasshoppers and waterbugs are considered treats in Asia. In South Africa, some people roast termites to eat like popcorn. In Mexico, bakers make a cake from water boatman eggs. Chocolate-covered ants might be served at parties in North America.

What's That Insect?

Fill in the blanks with words from the box.
Then write the letters in the squares to find
out which insect pest loves to munch wood.

You may find all kinds of interesting insects on a family trip. Don't bring them home! An insect may become a big pest in a new place.

germs	soil
vegetables	honey
hatch	ants

1. Insects help fruit and __ __ __ __ __ __ __ __ __ __ grow.
   1

2. Some insects spread __ __ __ __ __ that make us ill.
   2 3

3. When insect eggs __ __ __ __ __, the babies climb out.
   4

4. We like to eat __ __ __ __ __ made by bees.
   5

5. Tiny __ __ __ __ can spoil a picnic.
   6

6. Insects make the ground, or __ __ __ __ , healthy.
   7

The ⬜⬜⬜⬜⬜⬜⬜
    4 1 2 3 7 6 5

What Is a Spider?

Like insects, spiders have a hard outside skin instead of bones. Spiders are different from insects in some ways. They have eight walking legs, not six. Spiders have two main body parts, not three. Spiders don't have wings or antennae.

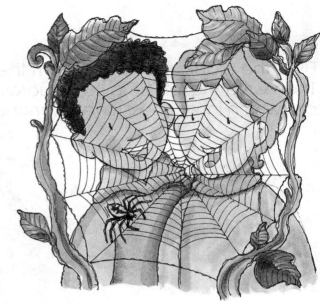

Spiders have parts that look like short legs.

The legs are connected to the front of the body.

The **abdomen** is the back part of the body.

Most spiders have eight eyes.

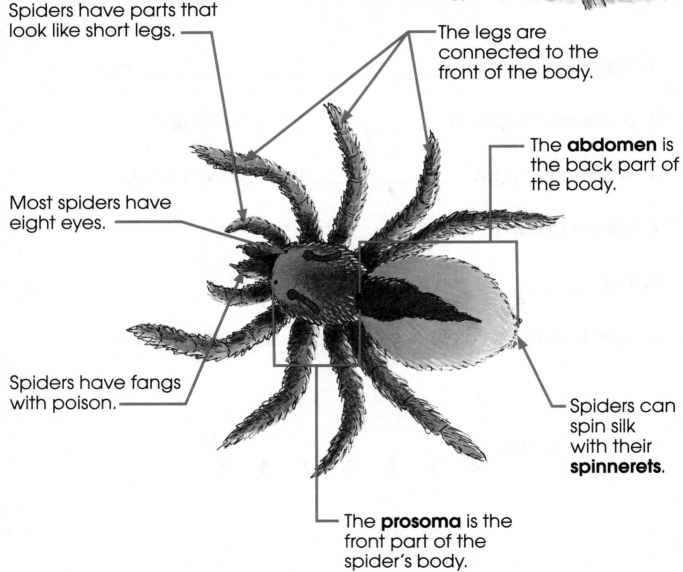

Spiders have fangs with poison.

Spiders can spin silk with their **spinnerets**.

The **prosoma** is the front part of the spider's body.

Spider Eyes

Most spiders have eight eyes, but some have six, four, or two. Even with all those eyes, though, spiders can't see very well. They rely on their senses of smell and touch. Many spiders feel things through the hairs that cover their bodies.

Look at the spider faces. How many eyes do you see? On the last spider, draw two, four, six, or eight eyes.

Which Spider Is Different?

The spiders in each row are the same, right? Wrong! Circle the spider that is different from the first one in each row.

Spiderwebs and Silk

All spiders make silk in their bodies. The silk comes out of the tail end of the abdomen.

Some spiders use these thin, but strong threads to make webs. Webs trap insects and other small animals for the spider to eat.

Some baby spiders use their own silk to leave the egg. The baby climbs to a high place. Then it lets out a line of silk into the wind. The wind pulls the silk, and the spider is carried off. This way of traveling is called **ballooning**.

Most spiders wrap their eggs in silk. The silk makes a tight, soft bag called an **egg sac**.

Other spiders let out a line of silk as they hunt. Then, if the spider falls, it is saved by the silk. Silk used in this way is called a **dragline**.

Spiderweb Puzzle

Use the clues to fill in the puzzle.

silk	poison
insects	eight
spinnerets	two

Across

2. A spider's _____ make silk.

5. A spider's fangs hold _____.

6. You may find _____ in a web.

Down

1. Webs are made of _____.

3. A spider has _____ legs.

4. A spider's body has _____ parts.

Web Detective

In the early morning, spiderwebs have tiny drops of dew, or water, on them. The drops sparkle in the sun and make the webs easy to see. You can make some "dew" with a spray bottle filled with water.

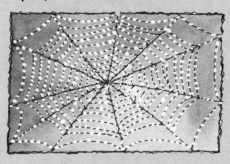

Take a walk with an adult in a park or a grassy field. Take a spray bottle, a notebook, and a pencil. Look for webs between the stems of tall flowers and grasses. Look between rocks and the ground, too. When you find a web, spray it gently with water. Draw or write what you see.

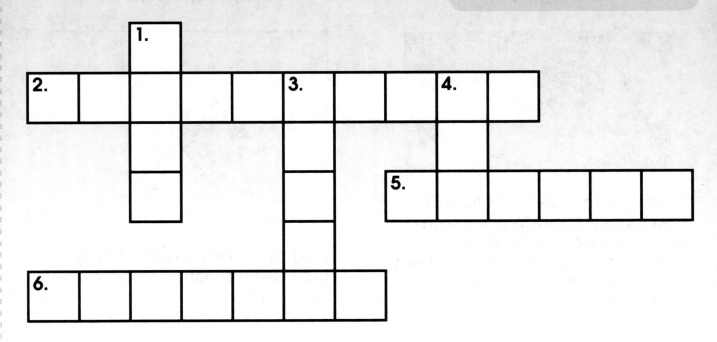

Kinds of Spiders

One way to group spiders is by how they catch their food. Web-spinning spiders wait for flying insects to get stuck in their webs. Hunting spiders chase insects or hide and wait for them to go by. Here are some examples of both kinds.

Web-Spinning Spiders

These spiders are easy to find. They make fancy webs that look like wagon wheels. These kinds of webs are **orb webs**. The garden spider's orb web can be over two feet around. Insects get trapped in the sticky web.

Cobweb Spiders

Did you ever look up at the ceiling and see dust-covered threads hanging down? Those are the tangled silk webs of cobweb spiders. The cobwebs catch dust. They catch flies, too.

Hunting Spiders

These spiders are hard to find. They slowly change color from white to yellow to match the flowers in which they hide. When a bee comes along, this crab spider grabs it.

Jumping Spiders

A jumping spider walks slowly and then runs and jumps to catch its food.

Break the Spider Code!

Use the code to figure out the spider's message.

Awesome!
Spiders' eyes are like tiny mirrors. They reflect the light from a flashlight at night.

A = 2	B = 4	C = 6	D = 8	E = 10	F = 12
G = 14	H = 16	I = 18	J = 20	K = 22	L = 24	M = 26
N = 28	O = 30	P = 32	Q = 34	R = 36	S = 38	T = 40
U = 42	V = 44	W = 46	X = 48	Y = 50	Z = 52

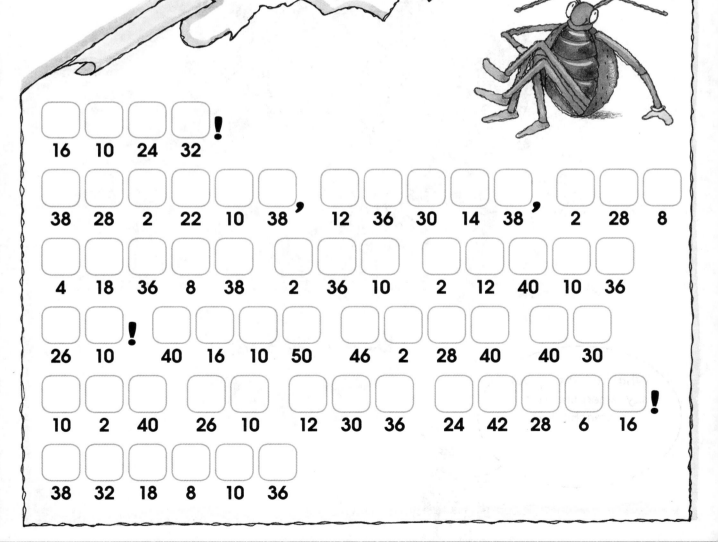

16 10 24 32 !

38 28 2 22 10 38 , 12 36 30 14 38 , 2 28 8

4 18 36 8 38 2 36 10 2 12 40 10 36

26 10 ! 40 16 10 50 46 2 28 40 40 30

10 2 40 26 10 12 30 36 24 42 28 6 16 !

38 32 18 8 10 36

What Spiders Eat

All spiders catch, kill, and eat other animals—most often insects. The spider sticks its fangs into an insect, and poison shoots into the insect and kills it.

Spiders cannot swallow chunks of food. So the spider puts liquids from its stomach into the body of the insect. The soft parts of the insect change to liquid. Then the spider slurps up the liquid food. The insect's hard outer skin is left over.

A few spiders eat other animals, as well as insects. Some spiders eat other spiders. Tarantulas, which can be as big as your hand, may even catch small birds, mice, and lizards.

What did the spider say when she got a stomachache?

It must have been someone I ate!

Suppose you have a restaurant just for spiders. What do you serve? Fill in the menu with delicious spider treats. Remember—spiders can only slurp, not chew.

Menu

Soups

_____

_____

Main Courses

_____

_____

Desserts

_____

_____

Drinks

_____

_____

**Discourage children from capturing spiders, because spiders may bite when cornered. Although most spiders' poison cannot harm humans, a few kinds can.

What Spiders Eat

Spiders and People

Spiders do people a favor by eating lots of insects that bug us. So don't bother spiders! Let them do their jobs.

People use spiders' silk in some surprising ways. Long ago, people used the strong silk to make fishing nets and traps to catch birds. Cobwebs were used as bandages. Today, very thin spider silk is used to make crosshairs in microscopes.

Think of something else for which strong, thin spider silk might be used. Write your suggestion on the lines.

_____

_____

A World of Insects and Spiders

Look at all the insects and spiders! Which ones do you remember seeing on other pages of this book? Color the picture. In the blank space, draw an insect or spider of your own.

More About Insects and Spiders

Information Books

Amazing Insects by Laurence Mound

The Big Bug Book by Margery Facklam

Bugs: A Closer Look at the World's Tiny Creatures by Jinny Johnson

Life of the Honeybee by Andreas Fischer-Nagel and Heiderose Fischer-Nagel

The Magic School Bus Inside a Beehive by Joanna Cole

Monster Bugs by Lucille Recht Penner

Who Eats What? Food Chains and Food Webs by Patricia Lauber

Magazines

ChickaDEE

Owl

Ranger Rick

Your Big Backyard

Storybooks

Antics! Cathi Hepworth

Charlotte's Web by E.B. White

The Grouchy Ladybug by Eric Carle

The Very Busy Spider by Eric Carle

The Very Hungry Caterpillar by Eric Carle

Why Mosquitoes Buzz in People's Ears by Verna Ardema

Reptiles and Amphibians Contents

What Is a Reptile? 92

Leapin' Lizards 97

Slithering Snakes 100

Talk About Turtles 104

Crocodiles and Alligators 106

Reptile Roundup 108

What Is an Amphibian? 109

Shy Salamanders 112

Fantastic Frogs 114

Hop Along Toads 116

Amphibian Fun 118

The Future of Reptiles & Amphibians 119

More About Reptiles & Amphibians 120

What Is a Reptile?

How is a box turtle like a python? A crocodile like an iguana? A chameleon (kuh-**mee**-lee-uhn) like a lizard? All these animals are alike in one important way—they are reptiles.

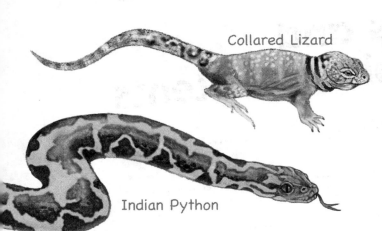

Collared Lizard

Nile Crocodile

Indian Python

You can see that reptiles vary greatly in size, shape, and color. Like many animals, including humans, reptiles are **vertebrates**—animals with backbones. And like people, they use lungs to breathe.

Eastern Box Turtle

How Many Reptiles

In this desert scene, all the animals are reptiles—except one. Circle the reptiles. Write the total number in the box.

Number of reptiles _____

Which animal is NOT a reptile? Look carefully!

_____

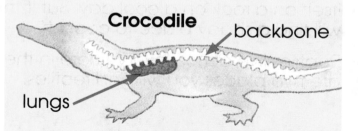

Look Inside!

Look at the crocodile's backbone and lungs. Then find those parts on the garter snake. Write **lungs** and **backbone** on the lines.

Reptile skin is dry and rough. The skin of lizards and snakes is made of overlapping scales. The scales of turtles and crocodiles grow into hard, bony plates.

Many kinds of reptiles shed their skin, or **molt**, several times a year. New scales grow under the old ones, and the skin loosens and falls off. Snakes crawl out of their old skin and leave it behind in one piece. Lizard skin comes off in big strips.

Their skin keeps water in reptiles' bodies for a long time. That's why so many kinds of reptiles can live in deserts and other dry places.

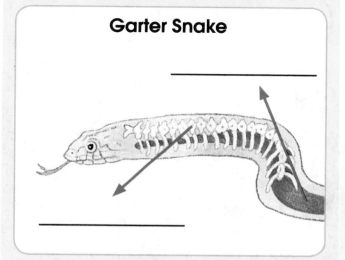

Crocodile

backbone

lungs

Garter Snake

_____

_____

Cool Word

A reptile's scales are made of **keratin**, the same as your fingernails.

Reptiles are cold-blooded animals. That means they have no built-in way to control the temperature of their bodies. When their surroundings are cold, they are cold. When it's warm out, they are warm. To stay alive, cold-blooded animals must not become extremely hot or cold. That's why you might see a snake sunning itself on a rock on a cool day. But if the day turns hot, the snake will find a shady place to cool off.

Reptiles live almost everywhere in the world, usually on land. Here are two places you will find reptiles.

Reptile Code

Put a letter in place of each number to finish the sentence. Then answer the question.

1 = C	2 = T	3 = A	4 = T
5 = R	6 = I	7 = N	8 = A

Snakes can be found on all continents except:

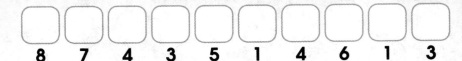

8 7 4 3 5 1 4 6 1 3

Can you guess why?

Most reptiles can see well. The kinds of reptiles that are active at night have long, narrow pupils, which can open very wide to let in as much light as possible. Reptiles that stay active during the day and sleep at night have round pupils.

Many reptiles can hear low sounds. Snakes can't hear sounds, though. They "hear" by feeling vibrations that travel through the ground. Most reptiles eat other animals. Some lizards and turtles eat mainly plants. Reptiles can go without food for a long time.

Stay Safe, Snake!

Help the snake get away from its enemies.

Complete the sentences with the words below.
Then write the words in the puzzle.

lungs	temperature
land	reptiles
backbone	plates

My tongue is really long. It's coated with sticky stuff that helps me catch prey.

Awesome!
There are more than 6,000 kinds of reptiles. Some are as tiny as 2 inches long. Others are longer than 30 feet.

Across

2. Reptiles breathe air through _____.

5. Cold-blooded animals do not have a constant body _____.

6. Most reptiles live on _____.

Down

1. Reptile skin is made of scales or bony _____.

3. An animal that is a vertebrate has a _____.

4. Turtles, snakes, lizards, and crocodiles are all _____.

Leapin' Lizards

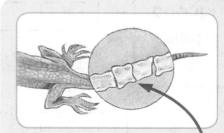

Green Iguana

The earliest lizards lived on Earth about 200 million years ago during the time of the dinosaurs, their reptile cousins. Lizards come in many colors and sizes. Most walk on four legs, but some don't have any legs at all.

Chilean Cave Lizard

Five-Lined Skink

Lizards defend themselves in unusual ways. Some have tails that break off when they are attacked. The tail wriggles around and distracts the attacker while the lizard escapes. Luckily, the tail grows back. Some lizards bluff. They puff up their bodies and hiss while lashing their tails. Some lizards change colors for protection.

Cracks in the lizard's backbone mark weak places where the tail can break apart.

Lizard Code

Put a letter in place of each number to finish the sentence.

1 = R	2 = T	3 = O	4 = I
5 = G	6 = M	7 = L	8 = A
9 = E	10 = N	11 = S	

Cool Word
Dinosaur means "terrible lizard." Unlike lizards, though, many dinosaurs walked on strong back legs.

The only poisonous lizard in the United States is the

◯ ◯ ◯ ◯ ◯ ◯ ◯ ◯ ◯ ◯ ◯ .
5 4 7 8   6 3 10 11 2 9 1

Most lizards eat insects, slugs (snails without shells), and other small animals. The chameleon uses its long, sticky tongue to catch insects quicker than you can say *flick!*

Big lizards, such as Komodo dragons, eat pigs, deer, and other large animals. Some lizards, iguanas for example, are plant eaters.

Awesome!
The world's biggest lizard, the Komodo dragon, can be as long as nine to ten feet and weigh nearly 300 pounds.

Puzzling Lizards

Complete the sentences with the words below. Then write the words in the puzzle.

slugs   iguana
dinosaurs   tails
tongue   four

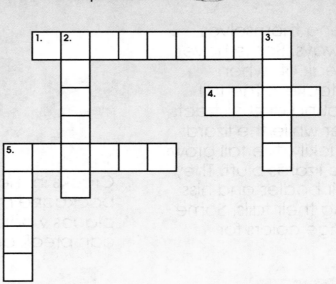

Across

1. Lizards lived during the time of the _____.

4. Most lizards walk on _____ legs.

5. A chameleon catches bugs with its long, sticky _____.

Down

2. One lizard that eats plants is the _____.

3. Some lizards eat _____.

5. Some lizards drop their _____ when they're in trouble.

Draco Lizard

Lizards really get around! Some swim and some fly—well, almost. A group of lizards called flying dragons glide from tree to tree the same way flying squirrels do.

Most lizards scamper about using their sharp claws to hold on to rough surfaces. One kind, the gecko, has slits on its toes that act like suction cups to help it stick to things. Geckos can walk upside down on a ceiling or a pane of glass!

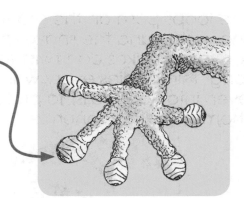

Some lizards that live on the ground, such as skinks, have very weak legs—or no legs at all.

Awesome!
How do you tell a legless lizard from a snake? Lizards have eyelids and ear openings. Snakes don't have either one.

Great Plains Skink

Guess the Lizard

Use the clues to write the names of the lizards.

| flying dragon   iguana   gecko   skink   komodo dragon |

1. I'm a real heavyweight. _____

2. Maybe I look like one, but I'm no snake. _____

3. My toes are the stickiest. _____

4. Let's eat a salad. _____

5. I glide through the air with the greatest of ease. _____

Slithering Snakes

What's the biggest difference between snakes and most other reptiles? Right! Snakes have no legs. Most slide along the ground by squeezing the muscles attached to their backbones so that their bodies make loops.

The loops push on the ground or in the water, and the snakes move forward. Snakes can twist their long, thin bodies every which way, even into tight balls, to protect themselves from enemies.

Indian Cobra

Corn Snake

Ribbon Snake

Horseshoe Snake

Word Find

Circle four places where snakes can be found. Look ↑, ↗, and ↘.

ground	water
land	trees

Z	T	I	K	Z	E	D
Q	S	R	A	R	E	N
D	D	R	E	L	R	U
E	N	T	H	E	V	O
L	A	F	R	N	S	R
W	L	O	Q	D	S	G

Awesome!

Snakes that live in deserts move by resting on their heads and tails and lifting the middle part of their bodies off the ground and swinging them forward in an **S**-shape. This movement, called **sidewinding**, helps keep their bellies off the scorching hot sand.

Snakes have a very good sense of smell that works in an unusual way. A snake's forked tongue flicks in and out constantly. This brings smells, such as the scent of animals to eat, or **prey**, into a special organ in the snake's mouth.

Viperine Snake

Other organs in snakes' heads sense temperature. A snake moves its head from side to side to notice changes in the air temperature. The heat-sensing organ helps snakes find and strike warm-blooded prey in total darkness.

What's Long and Green?

One of the longest snakes is the common anaconda. It can grow as long as 30 feet! Look at the graph.

Length in Feet

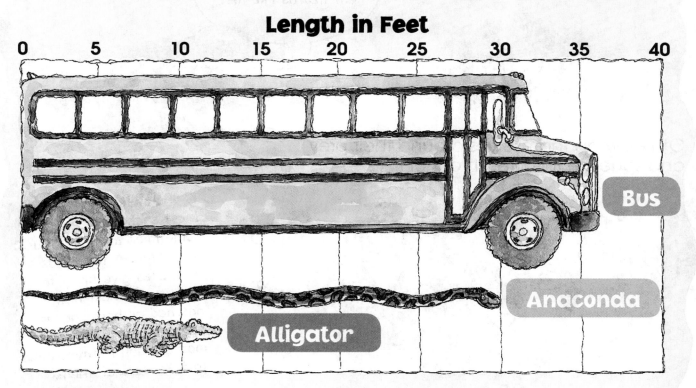

| 0 | 5 | 10 | 15 | 20 | 25 | 30 | 35 | 40 |

Bus

Anaconda

Alligator

1. About how many feet longer is the school bus than the anaconda? _____

2. How much longer is the anaconda than the alligator? _____

Snakes defend themselves in various ways. Their patterns and colors help some snakes blend with their surroundings. Others have bright colors and patterns that warn enemies to stay away.

Many snakes make warning sounds, such as hissing or rattling. A few kinds of snakes puff up, or **inflate**, parts of their body to scare enemies. Some snakes shoot poison, or **venom**, from their fangs into their prey to kill it.

Northern Copperhead

Eastern Coral Snake

Timber Rattler

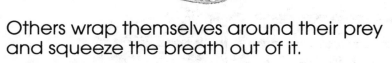

You mean snakes eat lizards like me?

Others wrap themselves around their prey and squeeze the breath out of it.

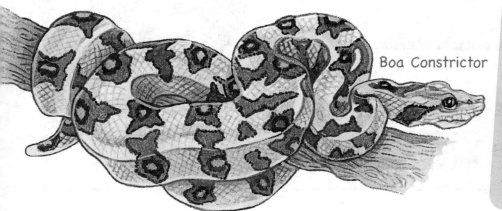

Boa Constrictor

Awesome!

Most snakes lay eggs, sometimes as many as 100 at a time. A few kinds of snakes give birth to live young. Most newly hatched or born snakes are on their own—their mothers don't stay around to take care of them.

Small snakes eat mice and rats, fish, birds, eggs, and small reptiles. Big ones eat large animals, such as goats or even alligators. Most snakes swallow their prey whole. Their jaws unhinge so their mouths can expand enough to fit the food through. Snakes can go for as long as a year between meals.

Snake Defenses

Match the defenses to the snakes.
Write the correct letters in the boxes.

A. **warning sounds**

B. **warning colors**

C. **protective colors**

D. **changes in shape**

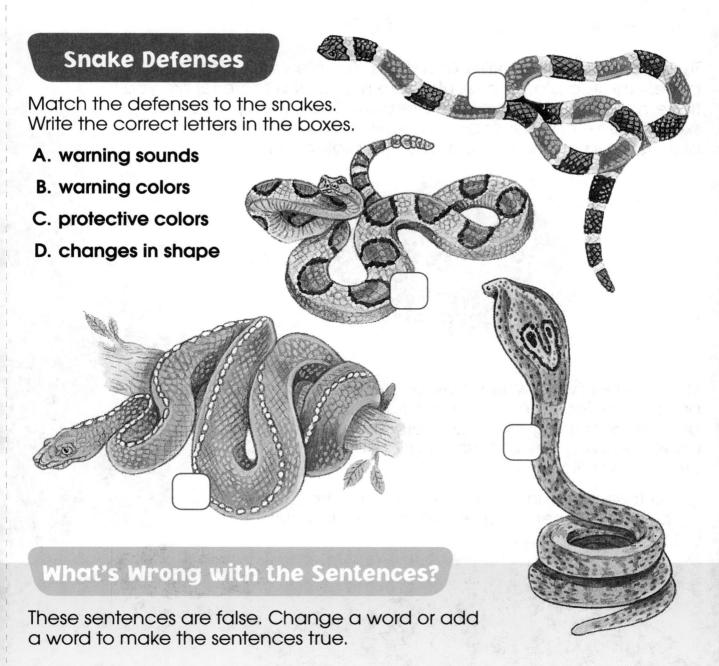

What's Wrong with the Sentences?

These sentences are false. Change a word or add
a word to make the sentences true.

1. The anaconda can grow as long as ten feet.

2. Most snakes take care of their babies.

3. Snakes that live in forests move by sidewinding.

4. Snakes use their fangs to sense smells.

Talk About Turtles

Turtles are the only reptiles with shells. A turtle's shell is made of plates. The top plates, or **scutes**, are made of a material like your fingernails. The bottom plates are bony. The shell is part of the skeleton, so it can never be left behind. When in danger, a turtle pulls its head and legs into its shell for protection.

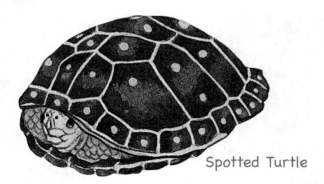

Spotted Turtle

Some turtles live in water most of the time, but they breathe air. Most kinds of turtles eat plants and animals. Snapping turtles are fierce hunters with powerful jaws. They eat fish, frogs, salamanders, and even baby alligators.

Tortoises are turtles that live only on land. They eat plants. Gopher tortoises eat grasses and fruits.

Painted Turtle

All turtles and tortoises lay their eggs on land. Many female sea turtles bury their eggs on the same beach where they were hatched. When the eggs hatch, the babies run for the water. Most of the babies are eaten before they get to the ocean.

WRITE NOW!

Imagine that you carry your home around with you as a turtle does. What is your house like? Write a description.

Turtle Race!

How many baby turtles do you see? _____

Awesome!

Turtles live longer than any other vertebrates, including people. A giant tortoise may live up to 200 years!

You can tell whether a turtle lives mostly on land or in the water by the shape of its shell. Most land turtles, such as the side-necked turtle, have high domed shells. Water turtles, the painted turtle is one, have flatter shells.

Side-Necked Turtle

Land or Water?

Predict whether these turtles live in the water or on land by the shape of their shells. Write **land** or **water** on the line under each picture.

1. _____   2. _____   3. _____   4. _____

Crocodiles and Alligators

You've probably seen crocodiles and alligators at a zoo or in pictures. Could you tell the crocodiles from the alligators? Their snouts and teeth are clues. A crocodile's snout is narrower than an alligator's, and it has a pair of bottom teeth that show when its mouth is shut. Both crocodiles and alligators live near water in warm parts of the world.

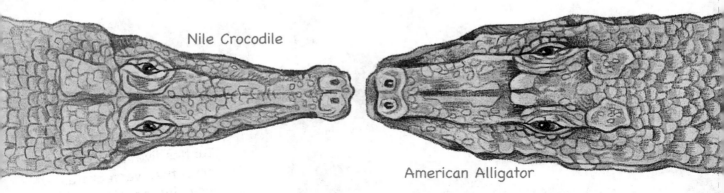

Nile Crocodile

American Alligator

Crocodiles and alligators have eyes, ears, and nostrils on top of their snout so they can hide themselves underwater as they hunt. Fast swimmers with strong jaws and big teeth, they eat just about any animal they can catch!

Awesome!

Alligators can weigh up to 1,000 pounds. Saltwater crocodiles can weigh as much as 2,000 pounds.

How many more pounds can crocodiles weigh than alligators?

_____

Like most reptiles, crocodiles and alligators lay eggs. The mother alligator guards the eggs until they hatch and protects the young alligators for a year or more. Some crocodiles guard their nests, too.

The Nile crocodile guards her eggs. After the eggs hatch, she carries her babies gently in her mouth from their nest on land to the river. The young crocodiles stay with her for several weeks before they swim off on their own.

Awesome!

Crocodiles cool off by resting with open mouths. They don't need to floss their teeth. Crocodiles let birds remove the food that's stuck in their teeth.

Help the mother Nile crocodile get her babies safely from their nest to the river.

Reptile Roundup

Awesome!

The tuatara (too-uh-tar-uh) looks like a lizard but is actually the last of a large group of reptiles that lived before the dinosaurs. Tuataras can be found only in parts of New Zealand.

Reptile Search & Sort

Circle the reptile names in the puzzle.
Then write the names of the reptiles where they belong in the chart.

anaconda	python	gecko
iguana	tortoise	chameleon
alligator	boa	

```
O  I  R  T  B  O  A  E  T  E
C  A  L  L  I  G  A  T  O  R
H  Z  N  R  S  U  D  H  R  B
A  D  G  A  R  A  E  B  T  R
M  R  E  Q  C  N  R  S  O  L
E  L  C  S  N  O  E  M  I  N
L  N  K  C  O  N  N  A  S  H
E  H  O  M  E  L  E  D  E  D
O  K  P  Y  T  H  O  N  A  N
N  A  T  I  G  U  A  N  A  B
```

Crocodiles & Alligators

Snakes

Turtles & Tortoises

Lizards

What Is an Amphibian?

Toads, frogs, salamanders, and some other animals are **amphibians** (am-**fib**-ee-uhnz). These animals are cold-blooded, have backbones, and as adults most kinds breathe through lungs just as reptiles do. But amphibians have lived on Earth much longer than reptiles. Amphibians have skin without scales. They live part of their lives in the water and part on land.

Cascades Frog

Scientists have divided amphibians into three groups. **Frogs** and **toads** have four legs and no tail, **salamanders** have long tails and two or four legs, and **caecilians** (suh-**sil**-ee-uhnz) have no legs and look like large earthworms.

Red Salamander

Caecilian

Leopard Frog

Frog Needs Help!

Lots of animals snack on amphibians. Help the frog escape from his enemies.

Alike and Different

Look at the circles with the words **Amphibians** and **Reptiles**. Write the letter for a way in which amphibians are different from reptiles under **Amphibians**. Write the letter for a way in which reptiles are different from amphibians under **Reptiles**. Where the circles overlap, write three letters for the qualities the animals share.

A. scaly skin   B. most breathe with lungs   C. skin without scales
D. vertebrates   E. cold-blooded

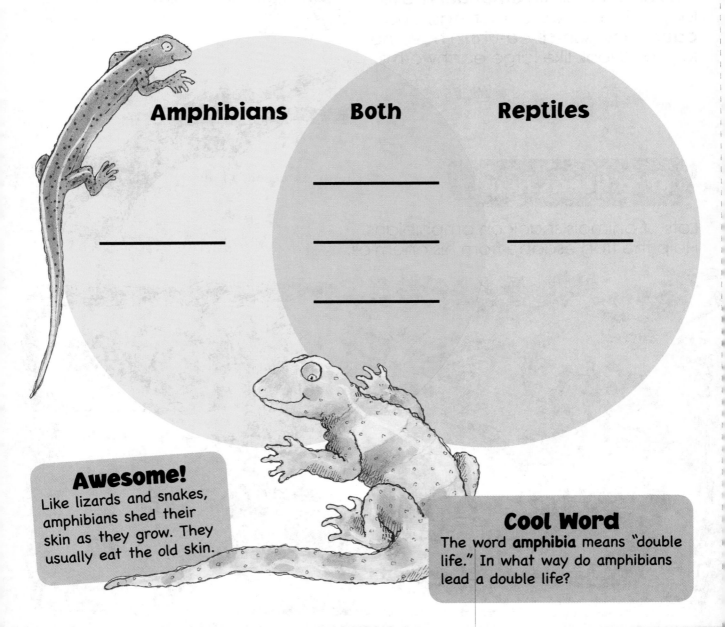

Amphibians   **Both**   **Reptiles**

_____

_____   _____   _____

_____

Awesome!
Like lizards and snakes, amphibians shed their skin as they grow. They usually eat the old skin.

Cool Word
The word **amphibia** means "double life." In what way do amphibians lead a double life?

Most young amphibians, or **larvae** (lar-vee), begin their lives in the water. They breathe through gills as fish do. Have you ever seen a tadpole? Tadpoles are the larvae of frogs.

Over time, two weeks to several months, the larvae grow and change into adults that look very different from the larvae. Most adults leave the water and live on land.

The Life of a Frog

Number the life stages of the frog in the correct order.

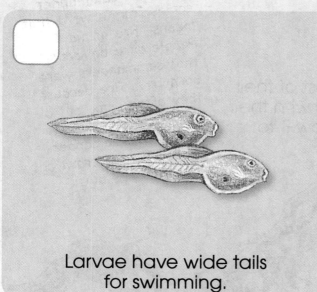

Larvae have wide tails for swimming.

Adult frogs live in and out of the water.

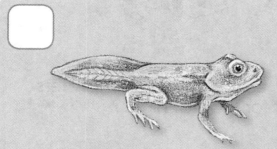

The tails of these larvae are shorter, and they breathe with lungs. Legs are growing and eyes are moving to the top of their heads. The larvae spend part of their time on land.

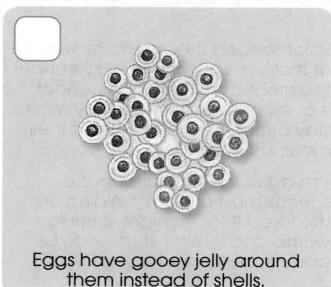

Eggs have gooey jelly around them instead of shells.

Shy Salamanders

Salamanders are shy animals that usually come out only at night. They look like lizards, except their skin is moist and smooth and their heads are rounder.

Italian Cave Salamander

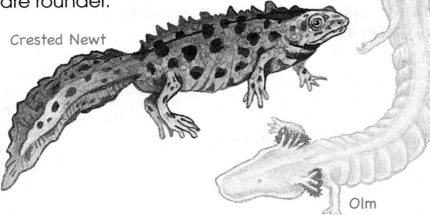
Crested Newt

Olm

Salamanders that live in water all or most of their lives can breathe through their skin and with their gills and lungs. The mudpuppy's gills allow it to breathe oxygen dissolved in water.

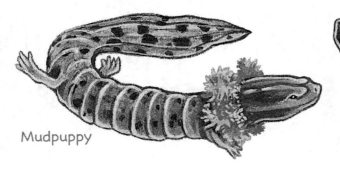
Mudpuppy

Spotted Salamander

Salamanders that spend most or all of their lives on land may live under the ground, in rotting logs, under leaves, or even in trees. They must stay out of the sun to protect their moist, sensitive skin.

The adult spotted salamander spends most of its time hiding on the forest floor. At night, it hunts worms and insects. It grows to be about nine inches long.

Why do you think salamanders hunt for food at night?

_____

_____

_____

Salamander Code

Help! I just lost a leg.
What should I do?

Use the code to answer
the question.

A = ▲   O = ✳   N = ◈   G = ◼   W = ◉

R = ✴   T = ★   E = ◎   H = ✥

| □ | □ | □ | □ | | □ | □ | □ | □ | □ | □ | □ | | □ | □ | □ | !
◼   ✴   ✳   ◉   ▲   ◈   ✳   ★   ✥   ◎   ✴   ✳   ◈   ◎

Would a Salamander Live Here?

Draw salamanders in the places they could live.

Fantastic Frogs

There are almost 4,000 different kinds of frogs, and they live in every part of the world except the frozen Antarctic. Frogs have smooth, moist skin the same as salamanders do, but their bodies are very different. Frogs have long, strong back legs for jumping.

European Green Tree Frog

River Frog

Ornate Horned Frog

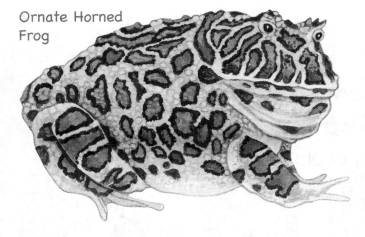

Common Bullfrog

Froggy Math

1. The biggest frog is the Goliath frog of Africa. It is about one foot, or 12 inches, long. The smallest kinds are only about 1/2 inch long. How much longer is the biggest frog than the smallest?

   _____

2. Many frogs can leap 20 times the length of their bodies. If a person four feet tall could do that, how far could the person jump?

   _____

3. The gliding frog uses its webbed feet to "fly" 50 feet through the air. How much longer is that than a 30-foot anaconda?

   _____

Gliding Frog

Most frogs' eyes are large. They are set at the side of the head so the frogs can watch all around for danger. Some frogs' skin is brightly colored to warn enemies to stay away.

Most frogs have colors and patterns that match their surroundings. This **camouflage** (**kam**-uh-flahzh) helps them hide from animals that want to eat them. Here's one example: The Asian leaf frog lives on forest floors. Its brown-and-yellow coloring and flat, pointy body make it look like a dead leaf.

Asian Leaf Frog

Hide & Seek

How many frogs can you find in this picture? Circle them.

Hop Along Toads

Toads look quite a bit like frogs, but they are different in some ways. Toads have dry, bumpy skin, not smooth, moist skin. They have plumper bodies and shorter back legs than frogs do. Because their legs are short, they can't leap like frogs. Instead, most toads hop.

Midwife Toad

Green Toad

Giant Toad

Yosemite Toad

Awesome!
Some people believe that if you touch a toad you'll get warts. You don't have to be a toad expert to know that isn't true!

Toads grow up in water, but most kinds spend much of their lives on land. Even land toads must keep their bodies from getting too dry. The spadefoot toad lives in hot, dry places. It keeps from drying out by burrowing underground. It may stay below the ground for months without eating. After a rainfall, it comes up at night and hunts for food.

Giant Plains Toad

Some male toads can puff up their throats to make noises that sound like flutes. Female toads can't do this.

Like frogs, many toads have long, sticky tongues that they use to catch worms, insects, and other small animals.

Toad or Frog?

Draw a line from each description to the correct animal.

Frog

smooth and moist

short legs

plump

hop

dry and bumpy

long legs

leap

thin

Toad

Amphibian Fun

Name That Amphibian

Decide which kind of amphibian is talking. Write its name.

| salamander | frog | toad |

I think hopping is more dignified than leaping.

1. _____

I'm shy. People used to think I came from fire.

2. _____

I can jump higher than anybody!

3. _____

Fact or Fiction

Write **true** or **false** after each sentence.

1. Frogs have smooth, moist skin. _____

2. Most salamanders come out at night. _____

3. Toads are better jumpers than frogs. _____

4. Some salamanders live in water. _____

5. Many frogs have bulging eyes to help them hide. _____

The Future of Reptiles & Amphibians

Although reptiles and amphibians have been around for millions of years, they may not last much longer in many parts of the world. Some reptiles and amphibians have already become **extinct**, or died off. These animals will never be seen again.

Here are some of the problems that threaten reptiles and amphibians.

- Air and water pollution caused by people is very harmful to these animals.

- Many reptiles and amphibians have lost their homes because people have built roads and houses where the animals lived.

- Many reptiles and amphibians are taken from their wild homes to be sold. Animals such as snakes, turtles, and salamanders usually die more quickly when they are kept as pets.

Action Plan

Make a plan to help reptiles and amphibians.

Write three ideas or steps of your plan.

_____

_____

_____

_____

_____

Awesome!
The International Union for Conservation of Nature is working to make conditions better for amphibians all over the world. Write them to learn how you can help.

IUCN Species Survival Commission, c/o Chicago Zoological Society, 3300 Golf Road Brookfield, IL 60513

Books

Reptiles by Mark Hutchinson

Salamanders by Nick Winnick

Alligators and Crocodiles by Gail Gibbons

Amazing Snakes! by Sarah L. Thompson

Nic Bishop Reptiles by Nic Bishop

Internet Resources

National Geographic Kids
www.kids.nationalgeographic.com/kids

San Diego Zoo
www.sandiegozoo.org/animalbytes

Video and Audio

Reptile by Eyewitness DVD

My Best Friend is a Salamander by Peter Himmelman

Birds Contents

What Is a Bird? 122

How Do Birds Fly? 124

How Wings Work 126

Best Beaks 128

Neat Feet 130

Nest Time 132

Plenty of Eggs 134

Bringing Up Babies 136

A Bird's Year 138

Bird Talk 140

Birds Travel 141

Where Do Birds Live? 142

Backyard Birds 144

Birds of Prey 146

Birds and People 148

More About Birds 150

What Is a Bird?

What do birds have that no other animals do? Feathers! Most birds use the feathers on their wings for flying. Feathers also help birds keep warm in cold weather.

Feel the bones in the middle of your back. These bones make up your backbone. Birds have backbones, too.

All birds begin life as eggs. Most mothers lay their eggs in nests they build. When the babies hatch, the parents feed them.

Which Animals Are Birds?

Almost all birds can fly.
But not all flying animals are birds.
Write a ✔ in the boxes by the birds.

A turtle lays her eggs in a nest that she digs. Her backbone is under the hard shell that covers her body.

Owls fly at night in search of mice. Their fringed wing feathers make no noise as they fly.

Awesome!

- The record holder for longest uninterrupted flight is the common swift who can stay airborne for up to 10 months at a time!

- The Arctic tern is the champion bird traveler. It makes a 25,000 mile round trip from the Arctic to the Antarctic and back.

Ducks swim by paddling their webbed feet. Oil keeps their feathers dry.

Remember!
If an animal has feathers, it's a bird. If it doesn't have feathers, it's not a bird.

It's a Fact

Birds are warm-blooded animals. The temperature inside their bodies stays about the same no matter what the air temperature is.

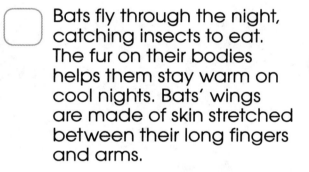

☐ Bats fly through the night, catching insects to eat. The fur on their bodies helps them stay warm on cool nights. Bats' wings are made of skin stretched between their long fingers and arms.

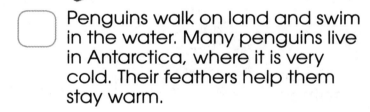

☐ Penguins walk on land and swim in the water. Many penguins live in Antarctica, where it is very cold. Their feathers help them stay warm.

☐ Flying squirrels have fur-covered flaps of skin between their front and hind legs. They use these flaps to glide from tree to tree.

Cool Words

The study of birds is called **ornithology** (or-nuh-**thol**-uh-jee). People who study birds are **ornithologists**.

☐ Butterflies have brightly colored wings. Instead of bones inside their bodies, butterflies have a hard covering on the outside.

How Do Birds Fly?

Birds are built to fly. Two things make them a success in the air: their low weight and their high power.

Low Weight

The whole bird except its legs, feet, and beak is covered with feathers. The **flight feathers** on a bird's wings and tail are light, strong, and flexible. Wing feathers fan the air so a bird can fly. Tail feathers balance and steer a bird.

Cool Word
Birds' feathers wear out and are replaced little by little every year. This process is called **molting**.

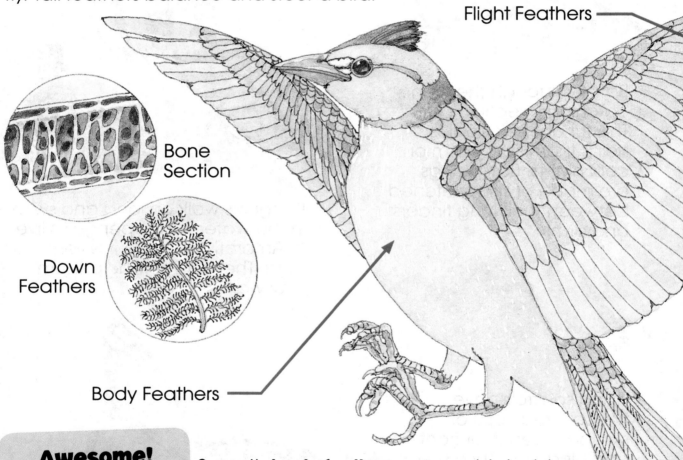

Flight Feathers

Bone Section

Down Feathers

Body Feathers

Awesome!
How do birds repair ruffled feathers after a rough flight? Tiny hooks hold flight feathers together. If a feather splits, a bird draws it through the beak and zips it together again.

Smooth **body feathers** cover a bird, giving it a rocket-like shape that moves easily through the air. Under their body feathers, birds have **down feathers**.

Soft down feathers trap the bird's body heat, keeping it warm even in very cold weather. Birds bones are thin and hollow, so they weigh less than other animal bones. Even though they are light, bird bones are very strong.

High Power

Birds eat foods that give them lots of energy—seeds, insects, worms, fish, and mice. They eat about one-fourth of their body weight a day. Birds burn up what they eat very quickly to get the energy they need to fly. Your body temperature is usually about 98.6°F. But a sparrow's body temperature is about 107°F.

Birds have air sacs connected to their lungs. They need extra air to get energy from food quickly and to cool off.

Many birds have huge breast muscles to power their wings.

It's a Fact

Birds take care of their feathers by fluffing and smoothing them with their beaks. Most birds' bodies make oil, and they use their beaks to spread body oil on their feathers to make them waterproof.

Birds Only

air sacs	tail	rocket
warmer	hollow	food

Fill in the blanks with words from the box. Then write the letters with numbers under them to find out what makes birds special.

1. A bird's body is ___ ___ ___ ___ ___ ___ than a person's body.
      1   2

2. Birds' bones are light because they are ___ ___ ___ ___ ___ ___ .
                                                    3

3. Birds need to eat lots of ___ ___ ___ ___ to get enough energy to fly.
                                  4

4. A bird's body is shaped like a ___ ___ ___ ___ ___ ___ .
                                      5   6

5. When a bird breathes, air goes into its lungs and ___ ___ ___ ___ ___ ___ ___ .
                                                                                    7

6. A bird uses its ___ ___ ___ ___ feathers to balance.
                       8

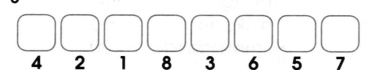

4 2 1 8 3 6 5 7

How Wings Work

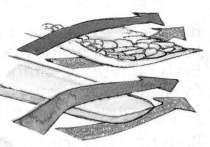

Bird wings are light, strong, and bendable. The inner part of a bird's wing is shaped like an airplane wing. It is curved on top, so air rushes over it and pulls away from the wing. The bottom part of the wing is straight, so air moves slower past it and pushes the wing up. When air pulls on top of the wing and pushes underneath, it lifts the bird up.

The feathers on the outside of a bird's wing twist and bend like a propeller when the wing flaps. This pulls a bird forward through the sky.

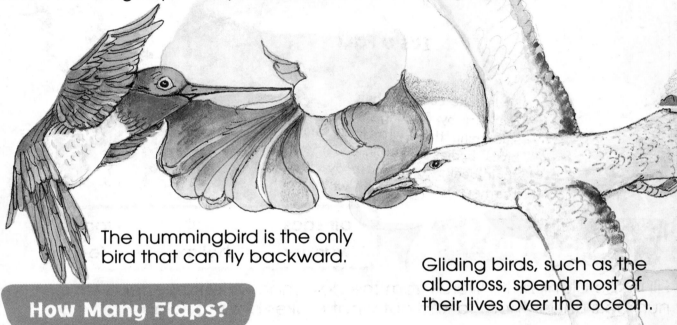

The hummingbird is the only bird that can fly backward.

Gliding birds, such as the albatross, spend most of their lives over the ocean.

How Many Flaps?

Can you flap your arms as fast as a bird can flap its wings? Ask someone to time you for ten seconds. Stretch your arms out straight and flap them up and down as fast as you can.

How many times did you flap your arms? _____

Compare your flapping speed with the speed of some birds.

Bird	Wing Flaps in 10 Seconds
Crow	20
Robin	23
Pigeon	30
Starling	45
Chickadee	270
Hummingbird	700

The kestrel can fly so slowly into the wind that it scarcely moves.

It's a Fact

At 1/10 of an ounce, the bee hummingbird is the lightest bird of all. Two other lightweights are the Humes ground jay and the least pygmy owl. They both weigh about an ounce. One big heavy bird is the great bustard, which can weigh 40 pounds.

kestrel	penguin
owl	chickadee
albatross	starling
hummingbird	pigeon
duck	

Where's My Name?

How many bird names can you find in the puzzle?

C	P	R	G	O	K	E	S	T	R	E	L
N	H	U	M	M	I	N	G	B	I	R	D
P	K	I	M	S	W	L	D	O	S	P	I
E	A	B	C	P	T	A	U	S	W	D	O
N	S	T	A	K	O	A	W	T	D	L	M
G	D	A	L	B	A	T	R	O	S	S	P
U	R	U	T	U	N	D	K	L	F	T	H
I	B	I	C	A	R	H	E	W	I	K	E
N	L	I	N	K	P	I	G	E	O	N	I
B	R	W	L	H	U	M	U	D	L	S	G

Best Beaks

When you eat, you hold your food in your hands or use a fork, knife, or spoon. How do birds eat? They have wings instead of hands—and wings are not good for holding food! But their beaks are specially shaped to help them eat their favorite foods.

Insect Picker

Warblers use their small, pointed beaks to pick insects from bark and leaves.

Meat Tearer

Hawks and owls have hooked beaks for tearing apart mice and other prey.

Insect Chiseler

Woodpeckers have long, strong beaks to drill into trees where insects hide.

Fish Catcher

A heron's long beak is perfect for stabbing fish and frogs.

Nectar Sipper

A hummingbird's long, narrow beak can reach into flowers to suck up sweet nectar.

Seed Cracker

Birds that eat hard seeds have short, cone-shaped beaks that can crack open tough seeds.

Water Strainer

Ducks use their flat beaks to strain water and filter tiny water plants and animals.

A Better Beak

You invite some bird guests to a spaghetti and meatball dinner. Invent a beak to help them eat. Draw a bird with this beak.

Awesome!

Pelicans scoop up fish with their large beaks. The bottom part of a pelican's beak is like a bucket made of stretchy skin. It can hold more food than can fit in the bird's stomach!

Feed Me!

Look carefully at these birds. Then draw a line from each bird to a food it eats.

Let's Eat!

Find the names of seven foods birds like to eat in the puzzle.

seeds	mice	insects	nectar
	fish	frogs	plants

P	A	G	N	S	C	R	L	F
F	M	P	D	E	L	L	P	R
R	I	N	S	E	C	T	S	O
N	C	S	I	D	I	T	E	G
D	E	F	H	S	M	E	A	S
S	G	P	L	A	N	T	S	R

How Many Fish?

Guess how many fish this pelican has in its pouch. _____

Now count the fish. How many are there? _____

How close was your estimate?

Neat Feet

Help! These birds have lost their feet. Birds' feet come in many shapes and sizes suited to the different places and ways they live. Can you find the right feet for these birds? Write the numbers in the boxes.

☐ This duck will sink without webbed feet to help him paddle around the pond.

☐ Don't let the robin fall off her branch! Find her perching feet with three toes in front and one toe behind for gripping tightly.

☐ The heron will sink in the mud without his long, wide toes.

☐ Even with her long, strong legs, the ostrich cannot race across the plains without her feet. Her two giant toes point forward for super-fast running.

☐ How can the woodpecker climb up a tree? With feet that have two toes in front and two toes in back to anchor him.

☐ This barred owl will starve without her feet! She needs long, curved claws, called **talons**, to grab mice and carry them home to eat.

Feathers, Beaks & Feet

Use the clues to fill in the words in the puzzle.

frogs   cones   molt   down   toes
straight   hummingbirds   oil

Across

4. Birds have _____ that keeps their feathers dry.

5. These birds can fly backward.

8. Ostriches have two big _____.

Down

1. Herons eat fish and _____.

2. These feathers keep birds warm.

3. The bottom of a bird's wing is _____.

6. When birds _____, they lose feathers a few at a time.

7. Seed-eating birds have beaks shaped like this.

Nest Time

Nests are safe places for baby animals to eat, rest, and stay warm. Many animals build nests, but birds are the experts. With their beaks, birds weave the materials they find into different shapes. Some birds use their feet to dig burrows for nesting. Many form their nests by pressing with their breasts.

Birds usually build nests near the places they find food. They may make nests in trees and bushes near your house. If you discover a nest, leave it where it is. Don't get too close. Taking care of eggs and baby birds is a job for bird parents—not for people.

Which Nest Is Which?

Read the clues and decide which nest belongs to each bird. Write the name of each bird under its nest.

Orioles weave nests that hang from tree branches.

An **elf owl** builds a nest in a cactus. The owl can't make the nest hole. It moves in after a woodpecker is done nesting.

Pigeons make simple nests of sticks on window ledges.

Woodpeckers drill holes in trees and make their nests inside.

Bluebirds make nests in holes in trees or fence posts. But they also build their nests inside bird boxes made by people.

An **ovenbird's** nest is hidden by the leaves of the forest floor.

3. _____

Weave a Nest

Many birds build the outside of their nests with sticks and bark. They line their nests with grasses, feathers, soft seeds, and animal hair. Some birds use mud as cement. When birds find bits of string, yarn, paper, or candy wrappers, they add them to the nests.

Build a nest with materials you find in your house and yard.

1. _____

2. _____

4. _____

5. _____

6. _____

Plenty of Eggs

After a pair of birds mates and builds a nest, the mother bird lays her eggs. Many birds lay a few eggs at a time. Seabirds such as albatrosses lay only one egg. Some ducks lay up to 12 eggs.

Birds that nest on the ground have speckled eggs that blend in with the surroundings. Owls, woodpeckers, and other birds that nest in holes have white eggs. These eggs are out of sight, so they do not need to be camouflaged.

Here an Egg, There an Egg

How many eggs can you find? _____

Cool Word
The eggs in a bird's nest are called a **clutch**.

Birds **incubate** their eggs—they keep them warm so the young can grow and hatch. Often both parents share the job of incubating the eggs. If the male is brightly colored, a cardinal for example, he does not sit on the nest. But he brings food to his mate while she keeps the eggs warm.

Some birds incubate their eggs for a long time. Albatrosses warm their eggs for 81 days. A bird that nests in your backyard will probably sit on its eggs for 12 to 14 days.

How Many Eggs?

Look at the chart. It shows some kinds of birds and the average number of eggs they lay at a time.

Bird	Number of Eggs
Barn Swallow	⬭ ⬭ ⬭ ⬭ ⬭
Blackbird	⬭ ⬭ ⬭ ⬭
Emperor Penguin	⬭
Emu	⬭ ⬭ ⬭ ⬭ ⬭ ⬭ ⬭ ⬭ ⬭ ⬭
Grouse	⬭ ⬭ ⬭ ⬭ ⬭ ⬭ ⬭ ⬭ ⬭ ⬭ ⬭ ⬭
Nightjar	⬭ ⬭
_____	

A pheasant lays 14 eggs.
Add this information to the chart.

Bringing Up Babies

What does a baby bird look like when it hatches? It depends on the kind of bird. Some babies are born with their eyes open and are covered with down. They leave the nest the day they hatch. Baby ducks and shorebirds follow their parents after they hatch, but find their own food. Chickens and grouse show their babies where to find food.

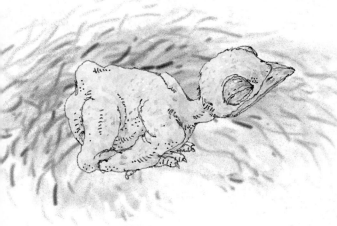

Other babies are born with their eyes closed and have no down. These babies can't leave the nest and must be fed by their parents. Both robin parents spend every minute of the day feeding their hungry young. For the first few days after hatching, mother robin also sits on the nest to keep her babies warm. After two weeks, the youngsters are finally ready to leave the nest. Then they follow their parents around begging for food.

This Way, Jay!

This blue jay has left her nest to find food. Her mate stayed behind to guard the babies. Help the jay find her way back to the nest.

Cool Word

Baby birds have a knob at the end of their beaks that helps them break out of their shells. This little knob is called an **egg tooth**. The egg tooth falls off when it's no longer needed.

Chirp Code

Baby bird has a message for you. Fill in the rest of the code. Then use the code to figure out the message.

A = 10	B = 20	C =	D = 40	E = 50	F =	
G =	H = 80	I = 90	J = 100	K = 110	L =	M = 130
N =	O = 150	P = 160	Q = 170	R =	S =	T = 200
U = 210	V = 220	W =	X = 240	Y =	Z = 260	

☐ ☐ ☐ ☐ ☐ ☐ ☐ ☐ ☐ ☐ ☐
90 200   90 190   70 50 200 200 90 140 70

☐ ☐ ☐ ☐ ☐ ☐ ☐ ☐ ☐ ☐ ☐ ☐ ☐
30 180 150 230 40 50 40   90 140   200 80 90 190

☐ ☐ ☐ ☐ ● ☐ ☐ ☐ ☐ ☐ ☐ ☐
140 50 190 200   230 10 200 30 80   130 50

☐ ☐ ☐ ☐ ☐ ☐ ☐ ☐ ☐ ☐ ☐ ☐ ☐ ☐
60 120 10 160   130 250   230 90 140 70 190   10 140 40

☐ ☐ ☐ ☐ ☐ ☐ !
60 120 250   150 210 200

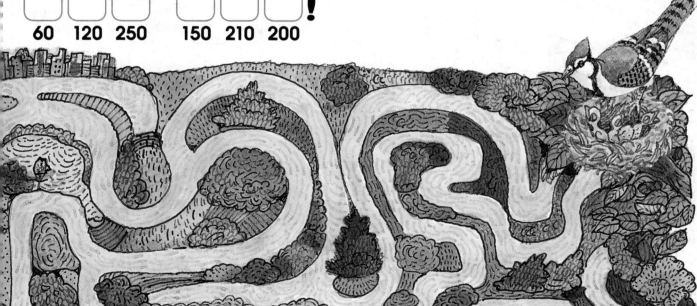

A Bird's Year

How do birds find enough food all year? This is what many birds that live near you do each season.

At first, parents are busy feeding their hungry babies. Later, they teach them to take care of themselves. There is plenty of food nearby. At the end of the summer, many birds molt.

Soon there will be lots of insects, worms, seeds, and berries to feed babies. Now is the time for birds to plan a family. Male birds choose an area, called their **territory**, with plenty of food nearby. A male sings and chases away other males that try to land on his territory. He lets female birds know about his special spot by singing and showing off. When a female joins a male, she chooses the best place for a nest.

Often birds fly together in groups, called **flocks**, during winter. With many eyes to watch for hawks and other predators, each bird in a flock can spend more time looking for food. At the end of winter, birds begin to migrate north where there will soon be plenty of food.

Soon birds won't be able to find insects, worms, and fruits to eat. Most birds in North America **migrate**—they fly south to warmer places so they can find enough food. Some birds, especially those that eat seeds, don't migrate. Many of these birds store acorns, grains, and insects in holes or cracks in trees so they will have food during the winter months.

A Bird's Year Puzzle

Use the clues to fill in the words in the puzzle.

| molt | find food | flock | territory |
| sings | migrate | fall | summer |

Across

2. Some birds _____ to warmer places.
4. a group of birds
5. A male bird _____ to attract his mate.
6. what birds must do all year

Down

1. season when there is plenty of food
2. lose old feathers and grow new ones
3. A male bird chases other males off his _____.
6. time when some birds store food

Bird Talk

From tiny peeps to loud screeches, birds call and sing to communicate. What do they say to each other? Baby birds tell their parents that they are hungry, scared, or hurt. Adults call to their mates or to groups of birds to warn them of danger. For most kinds of birds, only males sing.

Follow the Song

Help the female goldfinch follow the sweet song to find her mate.

Awesome!

Some birds, including mockingbirds and starlings, copy the songs of other birds. They imitate other sounds they hear, such as barks, whistles, and rumbles, too.

Birds Travel

Look at the map of North and South America. It shows the paths that some birds take when they migrate.

Migration Map

Phalarope

North America

Bobolink

American White Peican

Canada Warbler

Atlantic Ocean

Mexico

Sanderling

Central America

Pacific Ocean

South America

N
NW   NE
W   E
SW   SE
S

WRITE NOW!

You are a bird thinking about migrating. Write a list of things to do to get ready for your long trip.

Awesome!

- Migration takes a lot of energy. Some birds lose more than one-third of their body weight when they migrate.
- Migration can be very dangerous. Strong winds, storms, predators, starvation, power lines, tall buildings, and airplanes can kill migrating birds.

Use the map to identify the birds.

1. We winter in northern South America. _____

2. We make the longest trip. _____

3. We travel to Mexico. _____

4. We go to central South America. _____

5. Our trip is the shortest. _____

Where Do Birds Live?

Birds live all around the world in all sorts of places. They make their homes in deserts and on islands, in grasslands and forests, on farms and in cities. You can find birds in freezing cold polar regions and steamy hot tropics. Some birds never go far from water.

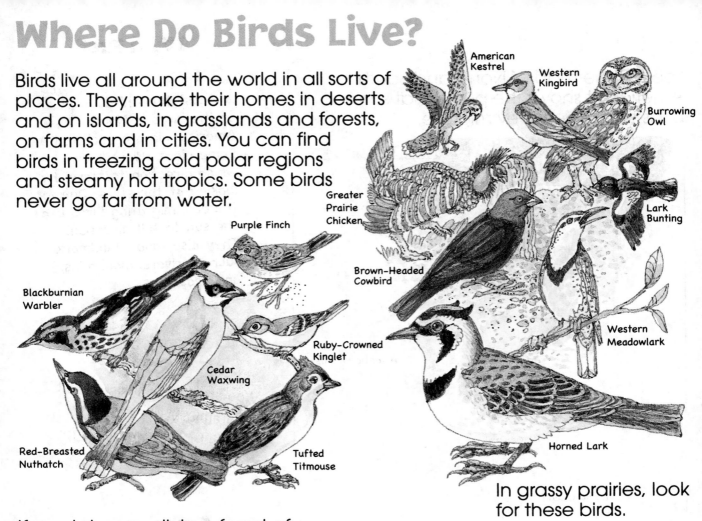

American Kestrel

Western Kingbird

Burrowing Owl

Lark Bunting

Greater Prairie Chicken

Brown-Headed Cowbird

Western Meadowlark

Purple Finch

Blackburnian Warbler

Ruby-Crowned Kinglet

Cedar Waxwing

Red-Breasted Nuthatch

Tufted Titmouse

Horned Lark

In grassy prairies, look for these birds.

If you take a walk in a forest of North America, you may see some of these birds.

Birds at Home

Where do these birds live? Write **forests, prairies, deserts, bushes,** or **water** on the line by each bird.

Here are some birds that live in deserts.

Golden Eagle

Cactus Wren

Elf Owl

Gambel's Quail

Greater Roadrunner

If you're near water, try to spot some of these birds.

Mallard

American Golden-Plover

California Gull

Common Tern

Spotted Sandpiper

Belted Kingfisher

Great Blue Heron

Common Loon

Northern Bobwhite

Brown Thrasher

Northern Mockingbird

Carolina Wren

Painted Bunting

These birds can be found in bushes and scrubby trees.

How Long Do Birds Live?

Bird	Average Number of Years
Starling	1½
Robin	1½
Bee Hummingbird	2
Kestrel	2
Blackbird	2½
Mute Swan	3
Swift	8
Emperor Penguin	20
Ostrich	40

Backyard Birds

Look for some of these birds in your backyard or close to home.

Where do house sparrows build their nests? Near people's houses, of course. A pair of house sparrows will nest in almost any little ledge or hole. Sometimes they nest in traffic lights or rain gutters.

What do you think a nuthatch cracks with its long, sharp bill? Nuts that it slips in the bark of a tree. This bird acrobat can climb headfirst down a tree and then turn around and go straight back up.

Why is that bird pecking a tree trunk? It's a downy woodpecker looking for insects and insect eggs to eat. Look for the red spot on the back of the male woodpecker's head.

It is easy to spot the bright red cardinal with the handsome crest on his head. The female cardinal is brownish, but she still stands out because of her red crest and beak. In the spring, you might find a pair of cardinals nesting in bushes.

Watch for gray colored juncos feeding on the ground under a feeder. When a junco flies, notice its bright white feathers on the outside of its tail.

In the winter, you might see goldfinches gobbling sunflower seeds. In the spring, the male goldfinch grows bright yellow feathers.

Ruby-throated hummingbirds look like flying jewels. They have squeaky voices, and their wings make buzzing sounds.

In the winter, the quick-moving chickadee spends many hours near feeders. Watch this little bird grab a seed, fly to a branch, crack the seed open, and eat it.

You are sure to find a pigeon in a park. You might notice a male pigeon ruffle his neck, bow his head, and turn in a circle. He could be bowing to his mate or keeping other males away.

Blue jays are so noisy you can hear them before you see them! To spot one, look for a big, bright blue bird with a blue crest. If you live west of the Rocky Mountains, you might see a Steller's jay.

"Cheer-up, cheer-up, cheerilee," sings the robin in spring. After a rainstorm, look for robins pulling up worms in the grass.

Who Am I?

Write the names of the birds. Then find the names in the puzzle.

| cardinal | pigeon | nuthatch |
| blue jay | robin | goldfinch |

1. I am big and blue.

   _____

2. I can climb down trees headfirst.

   _____

3. I have bright yellow feathers.

   _____

4. Will you feed me at the park?

   _____

5. I am as red as an apple. _____

6. I pull up earthworms from the ground. _____

```
C  P  I  G  E  O  N  P
I  A  U  O  C  R  B  H
F  G  R  L  A  F  L  G
N  P  O  D  P  C  U  O
R  A  H  F  I  T  E  U
O  G  T  I  U  N  J  L
B  J  D  N  R  I  A  C
I  Y  A  C  P  B  Y  L
N  U  T  H  A  T  C  H
```

Birds of Prey

Have you ever seen a hawk soar through the sky? Have you heard the booming call of an owl break the silence of a winter night? Hawks and owls are birds of prey—they hunt small animals and eat them. They catch mice, squirrels, rabbits, woodchucks, and even skunks. Some hunt small birds, frogs, snakes, fish, snails, and insects. Hawks hunt during the day. From high in the sky, a hawk can spot a small rabbit hopping in the grass. The hawk dives down, grasps the rabbit tightly in its talons, and brings the rabbit to a branch. There the hawk eats its meal with its hook-shaped beak and swallows the rabbit—fur, bones, and all.

Owls hunt at night. They have excellent hearing. When an owl hears the squeak of a far-off mouse, it flies silently toward the sound. The owl lands on a branch and turns its head to spot the mouse. Even in the dark, an owl can see a mouse scurry across a log. The owl spreads its huge feet and grabs the mouse with its talons. Then it swallows the mouse whole.

Inside a Pellet

After a hawk or owl digests its meal, it coughs up fur, feathers, and bones in hard pellets. By pulling apart a pellet, people can get clues about what the bird ate.

What do you think this owl had for breakfast?

_____

What did this hawk eat for lunch?

_____

Hawk or Owl?

Write **hawk**, **owl**, or **both** after each clue.

1. I hunt at night. _____

2. I catch animals with my sharp talons. _____

3. I see my food when I fly high in the sky. _____

4. I fly silently. _____

5. I can hear the squeak of a far-off mouse. _____

Birds and People

One way to get to know birds is to feed them. Put bird feeders where you can see them from a window—hanging from a tree branch, on the ground, or on a deck. Cats can hide in bushes, so place feeders a safe distance from shrubs. Be sure to provide water for the birds, too. In the winter, make sure the water doesn't freeze.

It's a Fact

The great auk was a seabird with wings so tiny it couldn't fly. People loved to eat auk eggs and flesh. They used oil from its body for fuel and plucked its feathers for hats. The great auk became extinct about 150 years ago. That means there will never again be great auks on Earth.

Pinecone Feeder

Tie a piece of string about 12 inches long around a pinecone. Spread peanut butter on the cone. Hang the bird feeder to a tree branch. If you like, before hanging your feeder, put some birdseed on a piece of waxed paper. Roll the peanut butter-covered cone in the seed.

Some birds are in trouble. The places they live, their **habitats**, are disappearing. People change marshes, swamps, and ponds to farms, parking lots, and housing developments. People clear forests to build shopping malls and roads. Tropical forests, the winter homes of many North American birds, are cut down and cattle ranches take their place.

Many people are trying to make certain that birds have the habitats they need to survive. Here is an example: Bluebirds used to be easy to find on farms and in towns. Then they started to disappear. Bluebirds make nests in holes in trees, but lots of their nesting trees had been cut down. Other birds, such as starlings and house sparrows, took over the few nest holes that remained. Then people found that bluebirds will nest in boxes in fields. Thousands of people built nest boxes and kept watch over the nesting birds. Now, more and more bluebirds are raising families in nest boxes.

Bird Words

Find out how many bird words you've learned.
Write the letter of its definition before each word.
Look back in the book if you need to.

☐ **call**	☐ **talon**	**A.** a long, curved claw
		B. the eggs in a bird's nest
☐ **incubate**	☐ **molt**	**C.** a group of birds
		D. one part of a bird's stomach
☐ **egg tooth**	☐ **preen**	**E.** to keep eggs warm so they will hatch
		F. a person who studies birds
☐ **flock**	☐ **song**	**G.** the knob at the end of a baby bird's beak that helps it get out of the egg
		H. a short sound a bird makes
☐ **gizzard**	☐ **clutch**	**I.** to use the beak to care for feathers
		J. to replace feathers little by little
☐ **ornithologist**		**K.** a series of notes that follow a pattern

More About Birds

Information Books

Birds in Your Backyard by Barbara Herkert

Birds, Nests, and Eggs by Mel Boring

Bird Talk: What Birds Are Saying and Why by Lita Judge

National Audubon Society First Field Guide, Birds by Scott Weidensaul

Olivia's Birds: Saving the Gulf by Olivia Bouler

Owls by Gail Gibbons

Storybooks

The Beauty of the Beast by Jack Pretlusky

Days of the Blackbird by Tomie dePaola

Loon by Susan Vande Griek

Make Way for Ducklings by Robert McCloskey

Owl Moon by Jane Yolen

Raven by Gerald McDermott

Magazines

chickaDEE

Owl

Ranger Rick

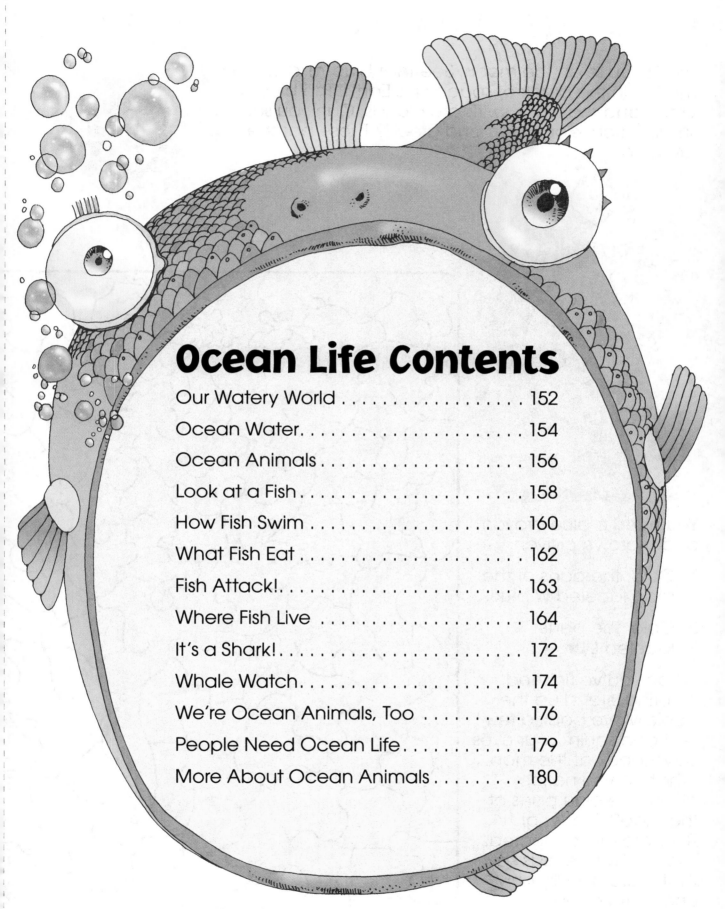

Ocean Life Contents

Our Watery World 152

Ocean Water. 154

Ocean Animals 156

Look at a Fish 158

How Fish Swim 160

What Fish Eat 162

Fish Attack!. 163

Where Fish Live 164

It's a Shark! 172

Whale Watch. 174

We're Ocean Animals, Too 176

People Need Ocean Life. 179

More About Ocean Animals 180

Our Watery World

Wow! You're on the moon. See that blue-and-white marble in the black of space? It's Earth. The blue is water and the white swirls are clouds. Can you see small patches of brown and green? Those patches are land.

Make a Map

You need a blue crayon and a brown crayon.

1. Color the parts of the map labeled **W** blue.

2. Color the parts labeled **L** brown.

When you've finished coloring, stand up the book. Move back a few feet and squint your eyes as you look at the map. What do you notice about the blue parts of the map? That's right! They are all connected. That's why scientists say that there is really only one world ocean.

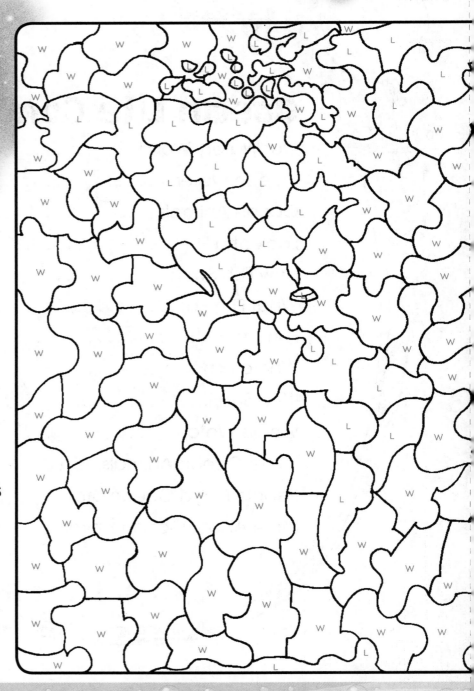

There is far more water than land on Earth. Almost three-fourths of Earth's surface is covered in water. And almost all of that water is in the ocean.

Write **water** and **land** on the correct lines.

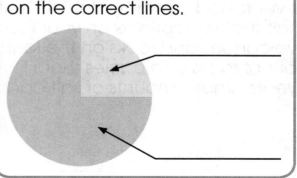

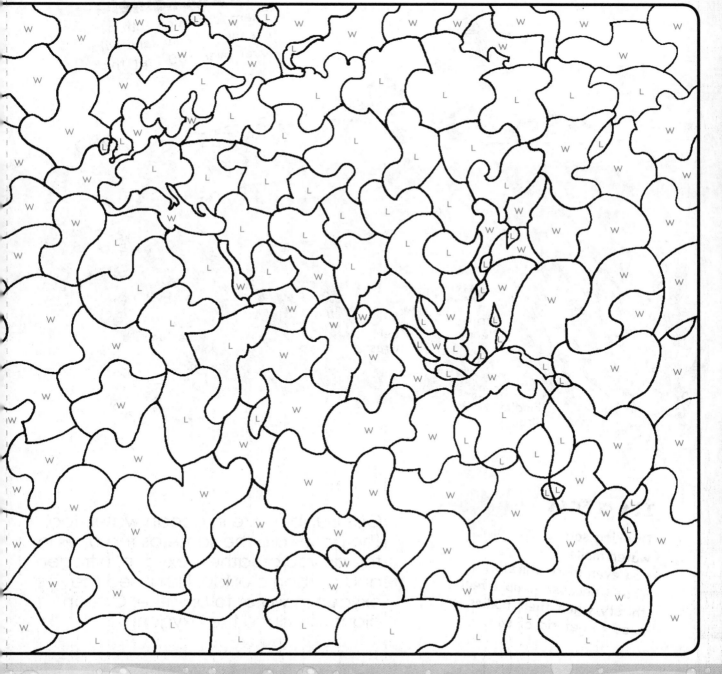

Ocean Water

Ocean water is different from the water in lakes and streams. Have you ever tasted ocean water? It's salty. Ocean water has the same kind of salt that you sprinkle on your food. The salt comes out of underwater volcanoes and rocks on the land. When it rains, the water wears away tiny bits of rocks and carries them in rivers to the ocean. After many millions of years, small amounts of salt add up to a very salty ocean.

Awesome!
There is enough salt in the oceans to cover land with a layer over 500 feet thick.

Striped Blenny

Eel Grass

Sea Lettuce

Fiddler Crab

It's a Fact

Drinking salt water makes you even more thirsty. That's because people feel thirsty when their bodies need to get rid of salt.

Gas bubbles are in ocean water, too. The gases are the same as the ones in the air you breathe—oxygen, nitrogen, and carbon dioxide. Fish need the oxygen in water to breathe. Ocean plants produce the oxygen.

Sinking & Floating

Swimming in the ocean is different from swimming in a lake. Is it easier to float in salt water or fresh water? Try this activity to find out.

You need a clear jar or mug, an egg, warm water, salt, and a spoon.

1. Fill the bowl or mug halfway with warm water.

2. Gently place the egg in the water. Describe or draw what happens.

3. Take the egg out of the water. Add a spoonful of salt and stir until the salt disappears. (It's still there, but it has dissolved.)

4. Put the egg in the water again. What do you see?

Repeat steps three and four until you see a change.

From what you have observed, is it easier to float in the ocean or in fresh water?

_____

Earth's Oceans: True or False?

Write **true** or **false** after each sentence.

1. Fish need to breathe oxygen. _____

2. Not much of Earth's surface is covered by water. _____

3. All the oceans on Earth are connected. _____

4. The saltier the water is, the easier it is to float. _____

5. Water in lakes is salty. _____

See! You've already learned quite a bit about oceans.

Ocean Animals

Close to shore or far from land, at the sunny surface or miles down in inky blackness, the ocean is filled with plants and animals. Most ocean animals are fish—there are about 20,000 different kinds—but other sorts of animals live in the ocean, too. Look at these ocean animals and the parts of the ocean where they live. Which of these animals are fish? It's not always easy to tell!

Seagulls

Flying Fish

Swordfish

Jellyfish

Halibut

Twilight Waters

Fish ID

Take a guess. Circle one of each kind of animal that you think is a fish. When you learn more about ocean life, turn back to this page to see whether you have changed your mind about any of the animals you identified.

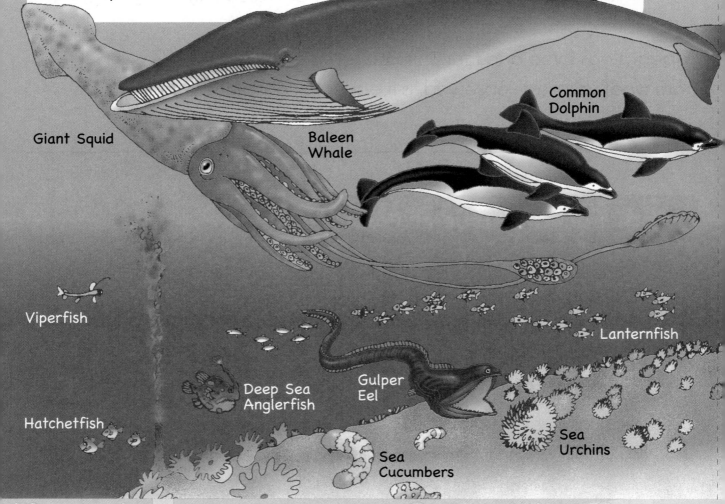

Giant Squid

Baleen Whale

Common Dolphin

Viperfish

Lanternfish

Deep Sea Anglerfish

Gulper Eel

Hatchetfish

Sea Cucumbers

Sea Urchins

Albatrosses

Sea Lions

Walruses

Mussels

Rockweed

Tidal Pool

Ocean Surface

Tuna

Skate

Cod

Octopus

Killer Whale

Loggerhead Turtle

Humpback Whale

Anchovies

Sea Pens

Manta Ray

Anemones

Basking Shark

Oysters

Midnight Waters

Sponges

Tripodfish

Tubeworms

157

Look at a Fish

What parts do nearly all fish have?

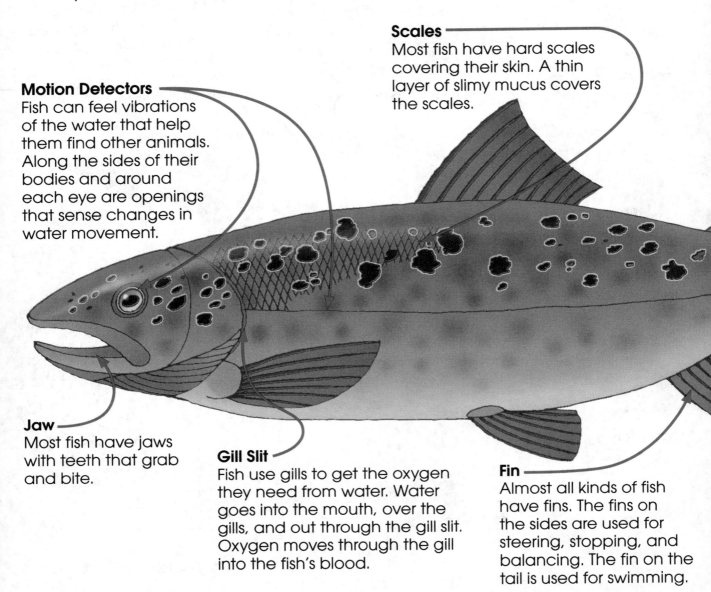

Scales
Most fish have hard scales covering their skin. A thin layer of slimy mucus covers the scales.

Motion Detectors
Fish can feel vibrations of the water that help them find other animals. Along the sides of their bodies and around each eye are openings that sense changes in water movement.

Jaw
Most fish have jaws with teeth that grab and bite.

Gill Slit
Fish use gills to get the oxygen they need from water. Water goes into the mouth, over the gills, and out through the gill slit. Oxygen moves through the gill into the fish's blood.

Fin
Almost all kinds of fish have fins. The fins on the sides are used for steering, stopping, and balancing. The fin on the tail is used for swimming.

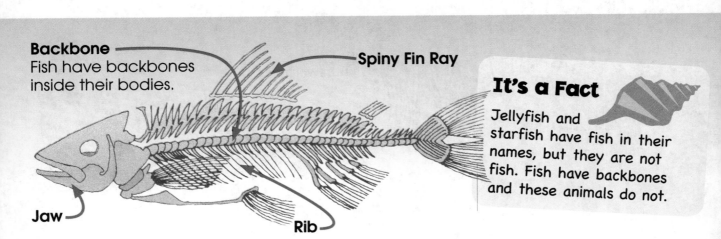

Backbone
Fish have backbones inside their bodies.

Spiny Fin Ray

Jaw

Rib

It's a Fact
Jellyfish and starfish have fish in their names, but they are not fish. Fish have backbones and these animals do not.

Albatrosses

Walruses

Sea Lions

Mussels

Rockweed

Tidal Pool

It's a Fact

Without sea plants there would be no animal life on Earth. The tiny ocean plants called **algae** (**al**-jee) make more than half of the world's oxygen, the gas needed for life.

Ocean Surface

Tuna

Skate

Cod

Octopus

Killer Whale

Loggerhead Turtle

Anchovies

Humpback Whale

Sea Pens

Manta Ray

Basking Shark

Anemones

Oysters

Midnight Waters

Tripodfish

Tubeworms

Sponges

Look at a Fish

What parts do nearly all fish have?

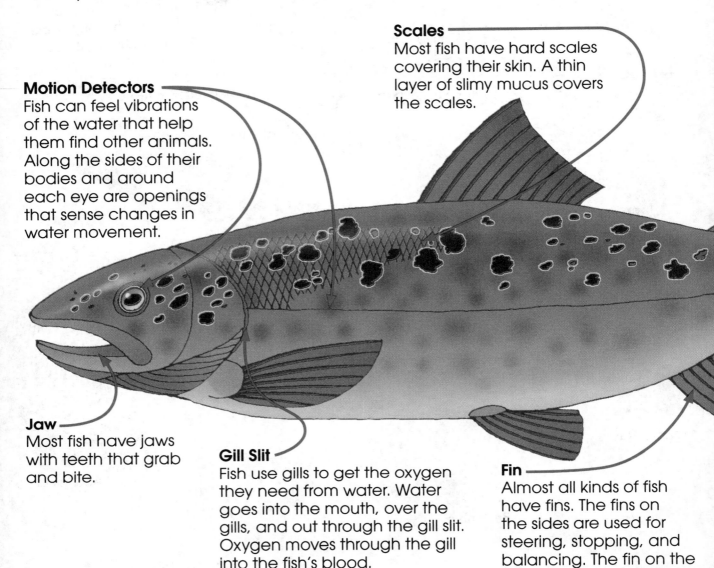

Scales
Most fish have hard scales covering their skin. A thin layer of slimy mucus covers the scales.

Motion Detectors
Fish can feel vibrations of the water that help them find other animals. Along the sides of their bodies and around each eye are openings that sense changes in water movement.

Jaw
Most fish have jaws with teeth that grab and bite.

Gill Slit
Fish use gills to get the oxygen they need from water. Water goes into the mouth, over the gills, and out through the gill slit. Oxygen moves through the gill into the fish's blood.

Fin
Almost all kinds of fish have fins. The fins on the sides are used for steering, stopping, and balancing. The fin on the tail is used for swimming.

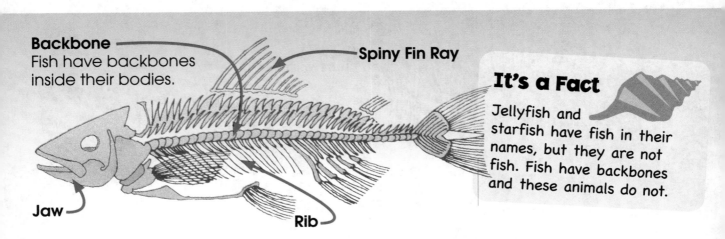

Backbone
Fish have backbones inside their bodies.

Spiny Fin Ray

Jaw

Rib

It's a Fact

Jellyfish and starfish have fish in their names, but they are not fish. Fish have backbones and these animals do not.

Backbone Code

Use the code to finish the definition.

B = 1   V = 2   R = 3   A = 4   E = 5   T = 6   S = 7

Animals with backbones are called

2	5	3	6	5	1	3	4	6	5	7

.

The Name Game

These names are funny, but all four are names of real fish. Draw what you think these fish might look like. Be as silly or serious as you want.

Lionfish

Butterflyfish

Nurse Shark

Lemon Shark

How Fish Swim

Most fish move forward by moving their tail fins as they curve their bodies from one side to the other. Fish "steer" with their side, or **pectoral**, fins. They stick out their left fin to turn left and their right one to turn right. To stop, they stick out both fins.

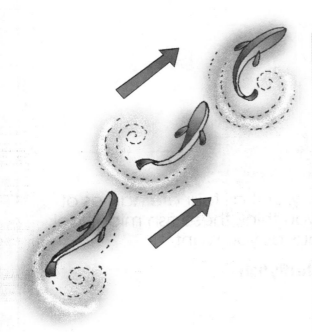

Herring are small fish that travel in groups, or **schools**, of thousands. The herring school is so tightly packed that it looks like one giant fish. Each herring stays in position by watching the fish to its left and right.

Fins Do It!

Which pilotfish is going faster?

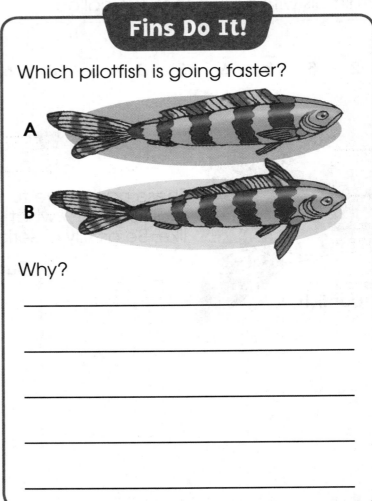

A

B

Why?

_____

_____

_____

_____

_____

_____

Some fish swim—and walk, too! A sculpin walks along the ocean floor on the tips of its side fins. A flying fish leaps out of the water to escape an enemy. It glides by stretching out its huge pectoral fins. A flight can last half a minute.

Flying Fish

Many fish can sink or rise when they want to. That's because they have pouches called **swim bladders** inside their bodies. Their swim bladders can fill up with gases and let out gases so the fish can float at any depth in the ocean. Without swim bladders, the fish would slowly sink to the bottom.

Make a Model Swim Bladder

How does a swim bladder work? Try this demonstration to find out.

You need a small plastic bottle with a tight-fitting cap, a sink, and water.

1. Fill the sink with water.

2. Fill the bottle with water. Tighten the cap.

3. Put the bottle in the water. Does it sink to the bottom?

4. Take away water from the "swim bladder" until it rises a bit. Keep pouring out water little by little until the bottle floats just below the surface of the water.

Put Away Those Fish!

You know that the more air a fish has in its swim bladder, the higher it rises in the water. Write the number of each fish at the depth at which you might find it.

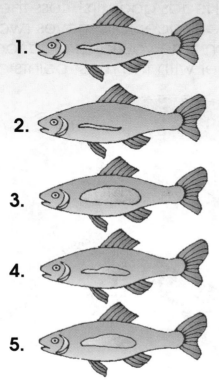

1.

2.

3.

4.

5.

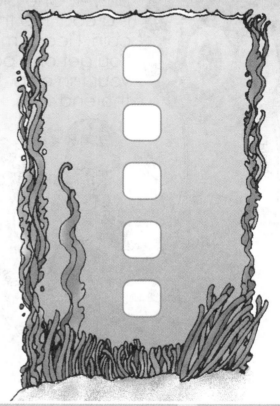

What Fish Eat

Some parts of the ocean look more like soup than clear water. That's because the water contains millions of creatures called **plankton**. Many plankton are so tiny you'd need a microscope to see them. Plantlike plankton make their own food from sunlight. Other plankton are animals that eat the plantlike ones.

Fish eat plankton. Some fish eat smaller fish. A few fish eat others of their own kind. Who eats what or whom in the ocean is called a **food chain**.

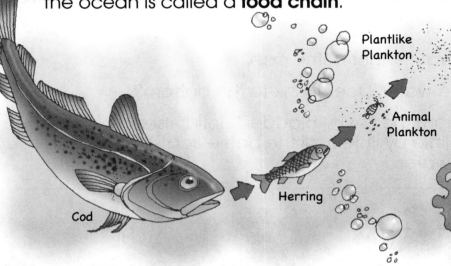

Plantlike Plankton

Animal Plankton

Herring

Cod

Fish Food

GO!

To play Fish Food, you need a coin and one other player. One player is a whale shark and the other is a cod. Flip the coin. Heads goes first. Toss the coin. Heads moves one space; tails moves two. You get one point each time you land on a food your fish eats. The player with the most points at the end wins.

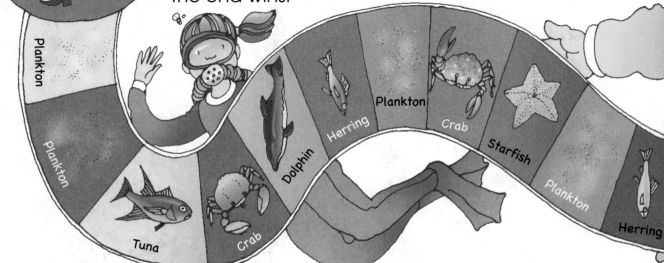

Plankton

Plankton

Tuna

Crab

Dolphin

Herring

Plankton

Crab

Starfish

Plankton

Herring

Fish Attack!

Ocean animals have many ways to attack and defend themselves, from great speed and a super sense of smell to electric shock and thick clouds of brown ink.

Sharks have huge jaws stuffed with sharp, pointed teeth. As their teeth wear out, they have several rows ready to replace them.

When the porcupine fish is attacked, it gulps water and blows itself up into a ball. Spines on its side stick out, making the fish a prickly mouthful.

If a fish comes too close, the sea cucumber shoots out sticky strands that trap the fish and give the sea cucumber time to escape.

The dragonfish has brilliant warning colors. Any animal that comes too close to its fins is jabbed with poison-filled spines. The stonefish hides on the ocean floor and injects prey with poison from its needlelike spines.

Awesome!

The biggest fish in the ocean, the 40-foot-long whale shark, eats plankton—the tiniest ocean creatures.

STOP!

Tuna

Crab

Plankton

Sea Cucumber

Plankton

Plankton

Crab

Nurse Shark

Herring

Clownfish

rring

It's a Fact

Waves sometimes glitter green at night. The green glow is light made by a kind of plankton called **diatoms**.

Where Fish Live

Close to Shore

Fish live in all parts of the ocean. The greatest number of fish live in the shallow water over the continental shelf, the land that slants down from the edge of the continents.

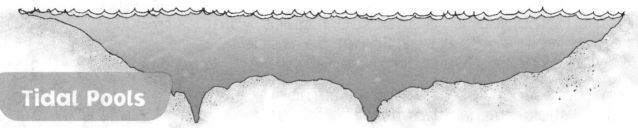

Tidal Pools

A tide is something like a wave, except that waves are moved by wind along the top of the water, and tides move from the floor and middle of the ocean, too. Tides are caused mainly by the pull of gravity from the moon. After a few hours at the beach, you'll realize that part of the beach is under water. That's the tide coming in. In a few more hours the water will move out again.

Pockets of water called **tidal pools** are left in rocky places on shore when the tide goes out. There's lots of life in tidal pools. Plants and animals have the food, clean water, and sunlight they need to live and grow. But they must be able to stand changes in water temperature and the pounding of waves.

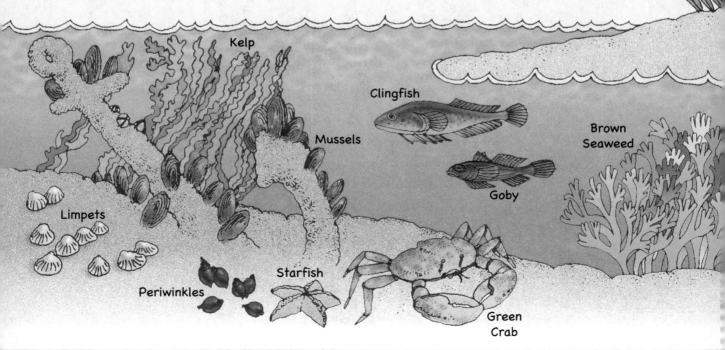

Kelp

Clingfish

Brown Seaweed

Mussels

Goby

Limpets

Starfish

Green Crab

Periwinkles

Plant or Animal?

Can you tell whether some of the living things in a tidal pool are plants or animals? Take a guess. Write the name of each living thing in the tidal pool under **Plants** or **Animals**. Check the answer page to see if you are right.

Plants

_____
_____
_____
_____
_____
_____
_____
_____
_____
_____
_____
_____
_____

Animals

_____
_____
_____
_____
_____
_____
_____
_____
_____
_____
_____
_____
_____

Bladder Wrack

Knotted Wrack

Sea Lettuce

Sugar Kelp

Barnacles

Anemones

Sea Snails

Coral Reefs

Look for coral reefs in warm, shallow ocean waters. The reefs grow on top of the skeletons of tiny animals called **polyps**. Coral reefs are home to lots of very colorful fish.

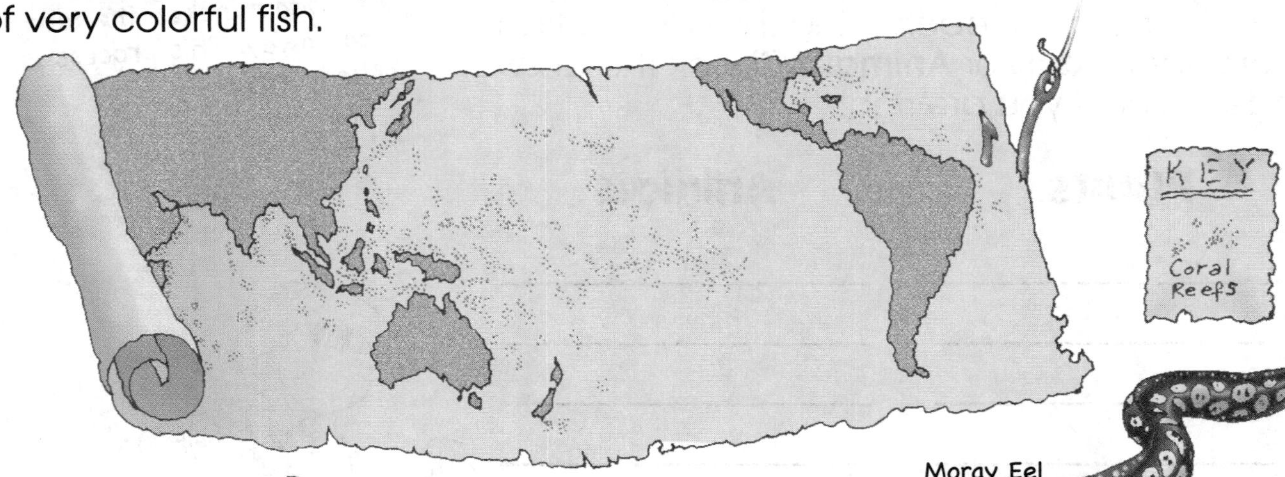

KEY

Coral Reefs

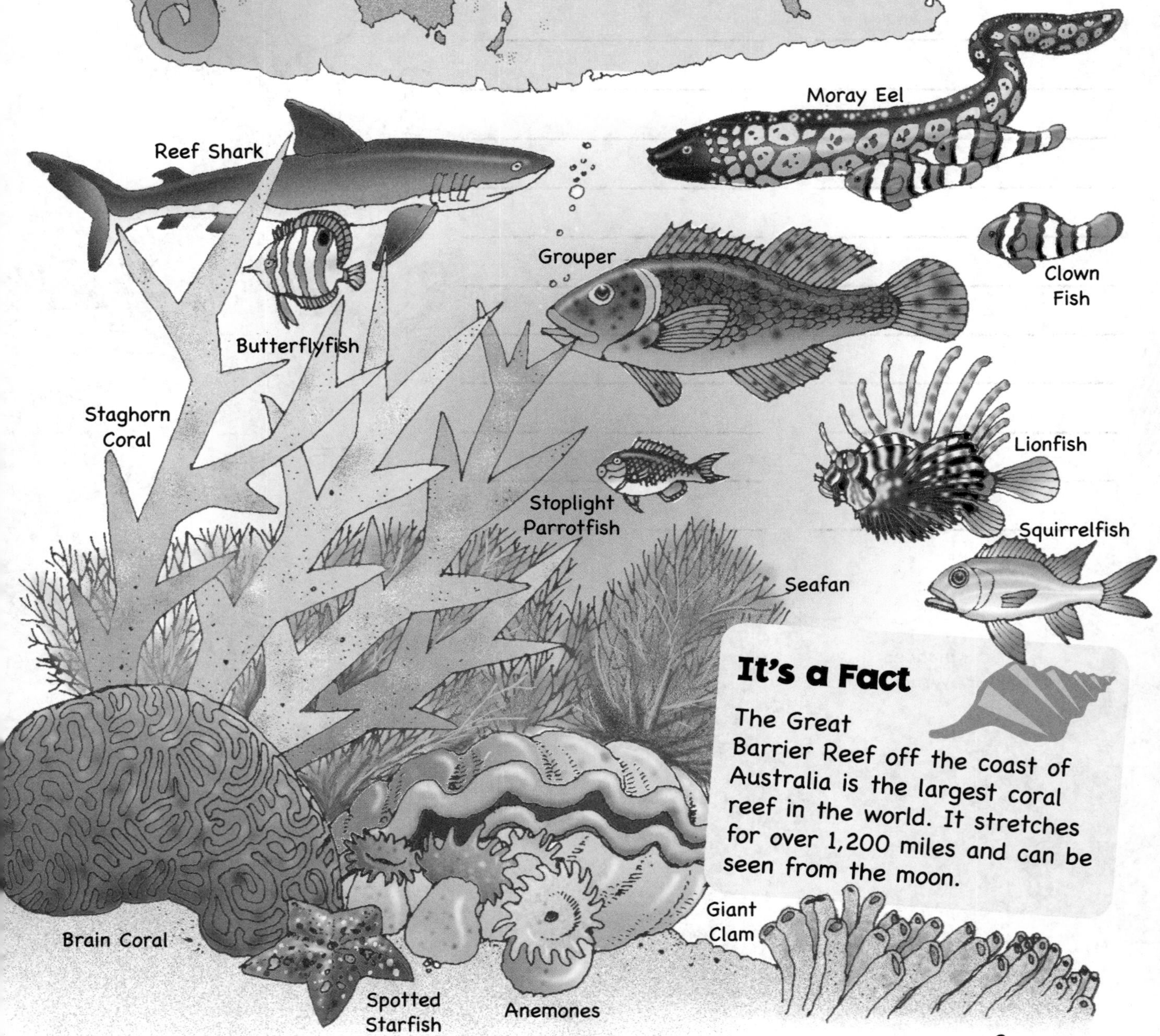

Moray Eel

Reef Shark

Clown Fish

Grouper

Butterflyfish

Staghorn Coral

Lionfish

Stoplight Parrotfish

Squirrelfish

Seafan

It's a Fact

The Great Barrier Reef off the coast of Australia is the largest coral reef in the world. It stretches for over 1,200 miles and can be seen from the moon.

Brain Coral

Giant Clam

Spotted Starfish

Anemones

Sponges

Fish Homes Puzzle

Use the clues to fill in the puzzle.

waves	roots	tidal pools
coral reefs	seahorse	rockfish
kelp forests	tides	polyps

Across

3. places off a coast where seaweed grows as tall as trees
6. a fish that doesn't look like one
8. Seaweed doesn't have _____ to take in water.
9. You'll find the most colorful fish here.

Down

1. These form when wind blows across the ocean.
2. a fish that looks like its name and stays near the ocean floor
4. When the tide goes out, ocean water is left here.
5. Skeletons of these tiny animals form coral reefs.
7. The moon causes the _____.

Scientists divide the open ocean far from land into three layers according to how much sunlight the water gets: the sunlight zone, the twilight zone, and the midnight zone.

Sunlight Zone

The sunlight zone is the ocean's top layer. It goes down about 300 feet, and the temperature is a pleasant 70° F. Even though it is the smallest zone, it has about 90 percent of ocean life. Sunlight brightens the water near the surface where plankton float. Bigger creatures also live in the sunny water. Some swimming animals cruise just below the surface. Some dive deep. Others break the water's surface to reach the air above.

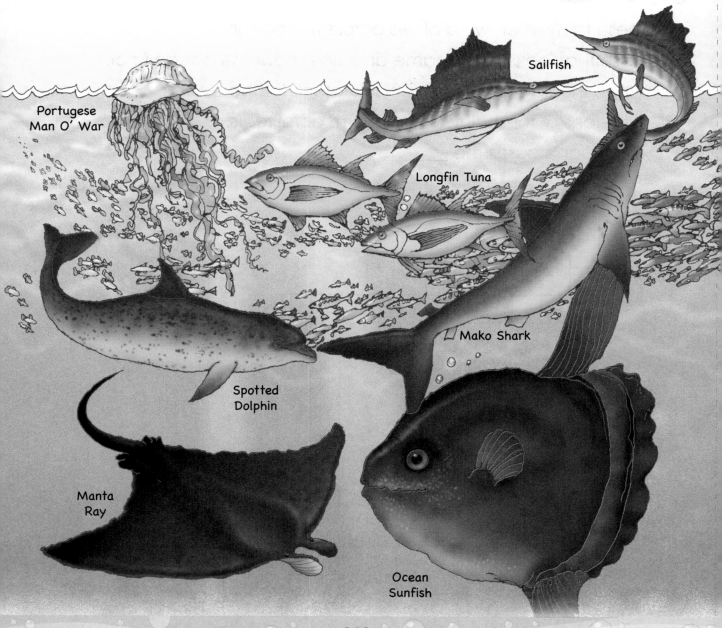

Portugese Man O' War

Sailfish

Longfin Tuna

Mako Shark

Spotted Dolphin

Manta Ray

Ocean Sunfish

168

Twilight Zone

The twilight zone extends from the bottom of the sunlight zone down about 3,000 feet. The water gets darker and colder—about 50° F. The fish that live here can't see very well, and there isn't enough light for plant plankton or seaweed to stay alive. Most food comes from dead plankton and animals that drift down from the surface waters.

It's a Fact

Some parts of the ocean move faster than others. These "rivers of water" are called **currents**. Currents are moved by winds that always blow in the same direction. Currents carry floating plankton from one part of the ocean to another.

Squid Code

Use the code to fill in the letters and learn about the size of the giant squid's eyes.

2 = A	4 = B	6 = E	8 = K
10 = L	12 = S	14 = T	

A giant squid's eyes can be as big as

4	2	12	8	6	14	4	2	10	10	12

Midnight Zone

The midnight zone goes from the bottom of the twilight zone to the floor of the ocean. This zone is dark and still. The temperature is really cold—about 43° F. The weight of the water from above presses very hard on the small, nearly blind animals that live here. Many deep-ocean fish have parts that glow from chemicals in their bodies. Their lights confuse enemies, lure prey, and attract mates.

At some places on the ocean floor, water as hot as 750° F shoots out of openings, or **vents**. Minerals collect around the vents to form underwater chimneys. The hot water rising from the chimneys looks like black smoke.

Shrimp

Devilfish

Giant Tube Worms

Ratfish

Awesome!

The very deepest parts of the ocean are cracks in the ocean floor called **trenches**. You could stack up to 26 Empire State Buildings and drop them into the deepest trench.

Clams

Sea Urchin

Rezone the Fish

Three of these fish are in the wrong zones. Circle them and draw a line from each circle to the zone in which each fish lives.
Look at pages 156, 157, 168, 169, and 170 for help.

Sunlight Waters

Twilight Waters

Midnight Waters

Deep Sea Anglerfish

Sea Spider

What Do You Think?

Fish in the deepest water are usually small. Most of them have very big mouths. Why might they look like this? Write your ideas.

_____

_____

_____

_____

_____

_____

_____

It's a Shark!

Sharks have terrible reputations. It's true that a few kinds of sharks, such as great white sharks, attack swimmers. But most sharks stay far away from people. Some of the hundreds of kinds of sharks are far too small—as small as five inches long—to hurt humans. Others are huge—as long as forty feet. Most sharks eat meat, and often that meat is other sharks.

Sharks are fish, but they don't have bones. Instead, a shark's skeleton is made of the same material as the tip of your nose and your ears. Sharks have streamlined bodies that help them glide through the water easily.

Sharks use their great hearing, vision, and sense of smell to hunt for food. They also use a sense that you don't have. All animals send out a little bit, or field, of electricity. Sharks sense this electricity through special tubes in their heads.

Tail

Second Dorsal Fin

Cool Words
The rubbery material that a shark's skeleton is made of is called **cartilage**. The shark's tiny, tooth-shaped scales are called **denticles**.

A-Mazing Sharks

A bull shark may swim from the ocean into a river or lake. Help this bull shark find its way back to salt water.

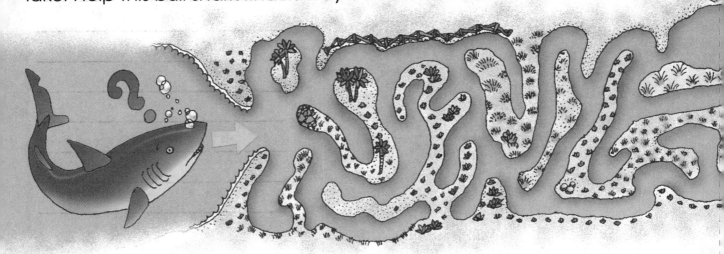

Tiger Shark

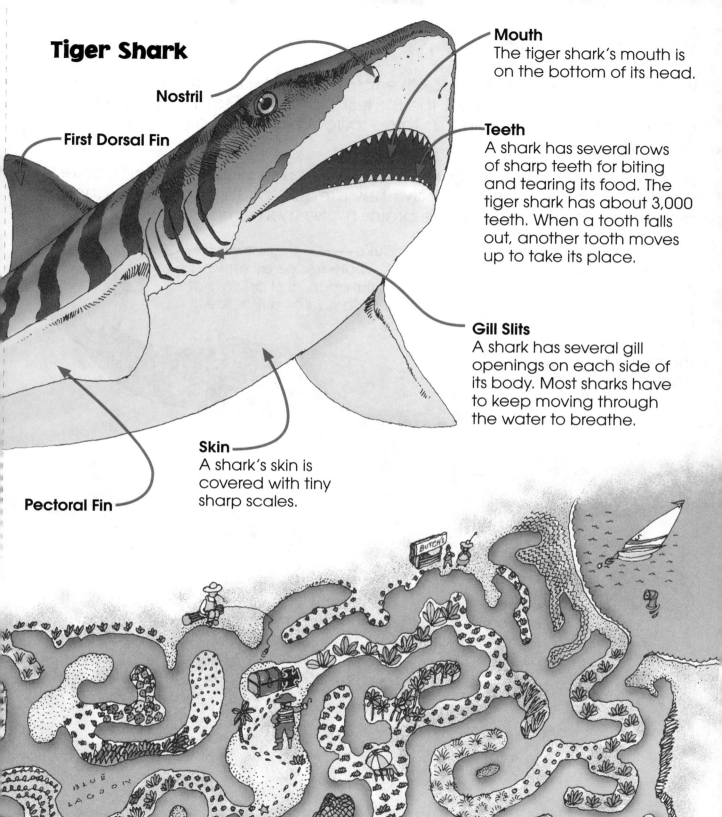

Nostril

First Dorsal Fin

Mouth
The tiger shark's mouth is on the bottom of its head.

Teeth
A shark has several rows of sharp teeth for biting and tearing its food. The tiger shark has about 3,000 teeth. When a tooth falls out, another tooth moves up to take its place.

Gill Slits
A shark has several gill openings on each side of its body. Most sharks have to keep moving through the water to breathe.

Skin
A shark's skin is covered with tiny sharp scales.

Pectoral Fin

Whale Watch

Whales and dolphins may look like fish, but they are actually huge mammals. The blue whale is the largest animal on Earth—100 feet long and 150 tons. That's as long as three railroad cars and as heavy as 30 African elephants!

Like all mammals, whales give birth to live young and feed their babies with milk from the mother's body. They breathe air through lungs, and they are warm-blooded. Their large brains make them smart.

Blowhole
A whale breathes through a blowhole at the top of its head. A huge cloud of moisture shoots out the blowhole when it breathes out.

Fluke
A whale travels by moving its flukes up and down, not side to side as a fish does.

Blue Whale

Common Dolphin

Baleen
Baleen is made from the same material as fingernails.

Fin Whale

Narwhal

Whales' bodies are suited to life in the ocean. Their streamlined bodies and smooth, rubbery skin help them slip easily through water. Whales can hold their breath a lot longer than you can. A sperm whale can wait 75 minutes between breaths.

There are two kinds of whales. Baleen whales have lots of thin plates called **baleen** in their mouths through which they strain plankton from the water. Toothed whales use their teeth to capture prey, but they don't chew it up. They swallow their prey whole. Dolphins and porpoises are two kinds of toothed whales.

Whales: Big, Bigger, Biggest

Use the whale graph to answer the questions.

Feet	10	20	30	40	50	60	70	80	90	100
Blue Whale										
Fin Whale										
Humpback Whale										
Pilot Whale										
Beluga Whale										

Beluga Whale

1. Which whale is the shortest? _____

2. Which whale is 80 feet long? _____

3. How much longer is the humpback whale than the pilot whale? _____

4. What is the difference in feet between the longest and shortest whale? _____

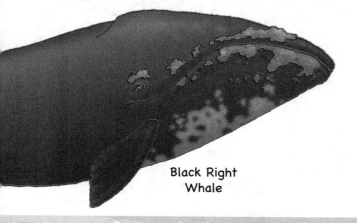

Black Right Whale

It's a Fact

Seals, sea lions, and walruses are ocean mammals, too. But unlike whales, they spend part of their lives on land.

We're Ocean Animals, Too

Jellyfish, Octopuses, and More

Quite a few ocean animals are **invertebrates**, animals without backbones.

Jellyfish look like clear, floating umbrellas. Not only do they lack a skeleton, they have no brain. All animals must watch out for a painful sting from the jellyfish's trailing arms, or **tentacles**.

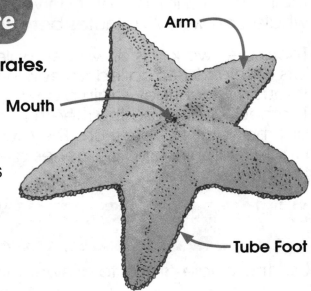

Arm

Mouth

Tube Foot

Mouth

Tentacle

The starfish is a spiny-skinned animal with pointed arms and a mouth and stomach at the middle of its body. It moves around using its tiny tube feet. A starfish's arms can drop off if something grabs them. Don't worry—the arms grow back.

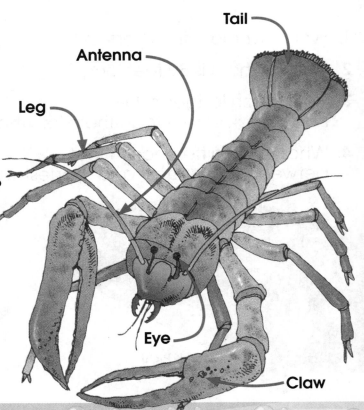

Tail

Antenna

Leg

Eye

Claw

Lobsters have hard shells on the outside of their bodies. Lobsters have to **molt**, or shed their shells, to grow. Do you think lobsters are red? That's after they are cooked. Most kinds of lobsters are dark green or blue with spots.

Lobsters are covered with tiny hairs that can sense the chemicals animals give off. That's how they find their food. They often eat animals that are related to them, including crabs and shrimp.

Like jellyfish, octopuses have tentacles, eight long arms with suckers on the bottom. They can creep along on their arms, but octopuses have a quicker way to travel—by jet propulsion. The octopus sucks water into its body and shoots it out through a narrow opening. The force of the water moves the octopus forward rapidly.

Eye

Sucker

Tentacle

Awesome!

A starfish eats when it takes its stomach out to lunch! The stomach comes out of the mouth in the middle of the underside, gets inside a clam shell, and slowly digests the clam.

Who Am I?

Write the number to match each clue with the animal it describes.

1. My eyes are at the end of long stalks.

2. My mouth and stomach are in the same part of my body.

3. I float on top of the water like an umbrella.

4. I can move really fast—but not as fast as a jet.

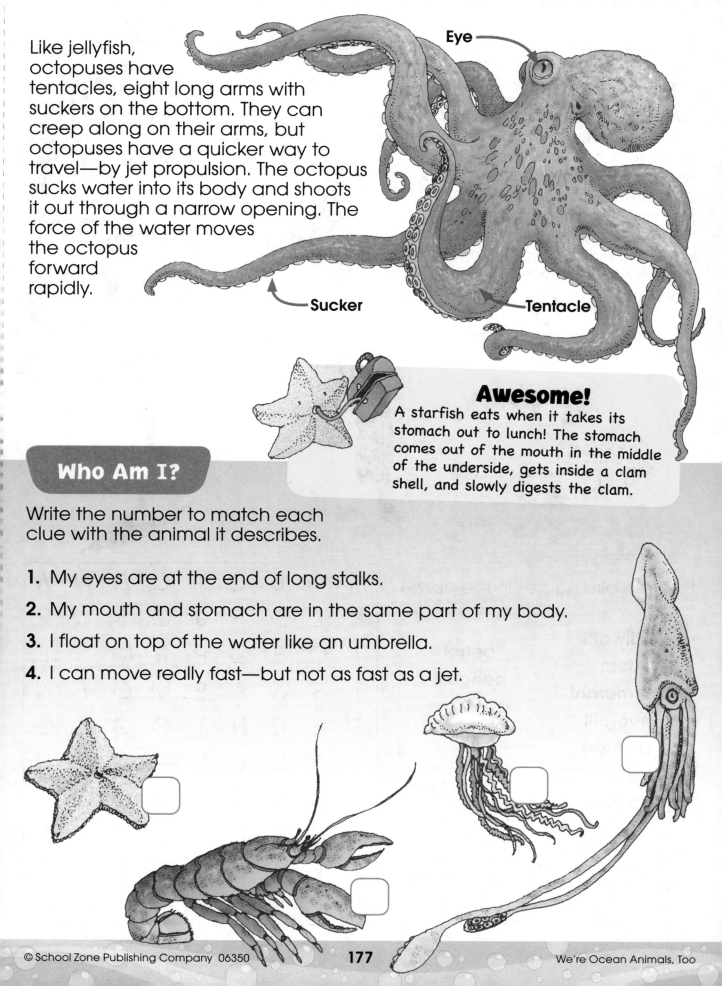

Ocean Birds

Lots of kinds of birds depend on the ocean for food. Some, such as pelicans, cormorants, and seagulls, stay along the coasts, and others hunt for food close to shore. Some offshore birds are penguins, puffins, and terns. You'll find albatrosses, petrels, and kittiwakes miles out over the open ocean.

Seagull

Cormorant

Puffin

Petrel

Albatross

Penguin

Pelican

Bird Word Search

Find the bird names in the puzzle.

kittiwake
tern
cormorant
seagull
pelican
petrel
penguin
albatross
puffin

A	P	E	L	I	C	A	N	W
K	L	D	F	J	O	S	W	P
I	C	B	Q	P	R	M	S	E
T	S	W	A	E	M	O	F	N
T	E	R	N	T	O	G	K	G
I	A	D	U	R	R	W	M	U
W	G	S	I	E	A	O	Q	I
A	U	Y	F	L	N	Q	S	N
K	L	J	F	U	T	B	X	S
E	L	P	U	F	F	I	N	Q

It's a Fact

The albatross is the biggest sea bird. Its long narrow wings are about twelve feet across. The shape and length of its wings help the albatross soar and glide in the strong winds over the open ocean.

People Need Ocean Life

Did you ever taste a clam, lobster, or salmon? Or order anchovies on your pizza? Then you eat ocean animals. Do you eat chicken? Often chickens are fed ground-up fish parts. Other foods, including ice cream, contain seaweed. Kelp is used as a fertilizer in gardens. Red algae is a medicine for blood. These are just a very few of the thousands of ways people benefit from ocean life.

People put things in the ocean that can harm fish and other ocean life. The worst kinds of ocean pollution are from human and animal waste (the kind you flush away) and chemicals. Garbage, including plastic bags and six-pack rings, often finds its way into the ocean. Ocean animals may eat plastic bags or get their heads caught in the rings of six-packs. What can you do? Most important, don't litter!

What a Mess!

Sometimes oil tanker ships leak oil onto the surface of the ocean. Currents and tides can carry the pollution from the ship. Ocean animals that get coated with the oil may die. Can you find a good way to clean up oil spills?

You need a small plastic container, water, vegetable oil, and sand or pebbles.

1. Put sand or pebbles in the bottom of the container—that's your beach.

2. Pour in a little water so that part of the beach is still dry.

3. Add a spoonful of vegetable oil—that's the oil spill.

4. Gently rock the container back and forth. The movement of the water is like waves at the shore. What happens to the dry beach?

5. Now think of ways to clean the oil from the beach and water. Try out your best idea and write about how it worked.

More About Ocean Animals

Storybooks

A House for Hermit Crab by Eric Carle

The Rainbow Fish by Marcus Pfister

Seashells by the Seashore by Marianne Berkes

Swimmy by Leo Lionni

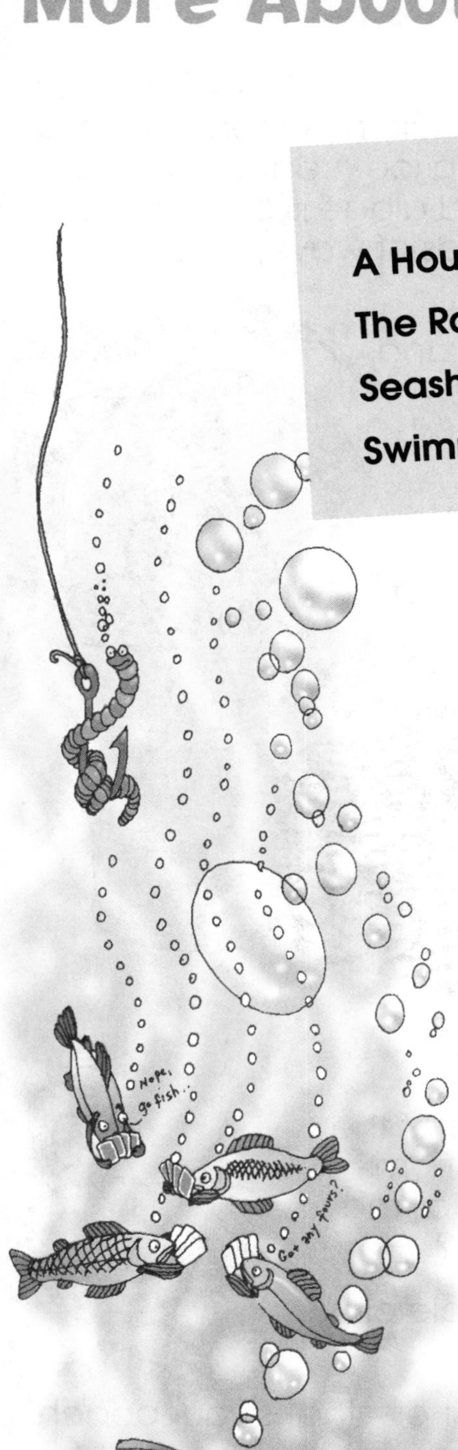

Information Books

The Aquarium Book by George Ancona

Exploring the Deep, Dark Sea by Gail Gibbons

I Wonder Why the Sea is Salty by Anita Ganeri

The Magic School Bus on the Ocean Floor by Joanna Cole

National Geographic Readers: Weird Sea Creatures by Laura Marsh

Night Reef by William Sargent

Ocean by Samantha Gray

Outside and Inside Sharks by Sandra Markle

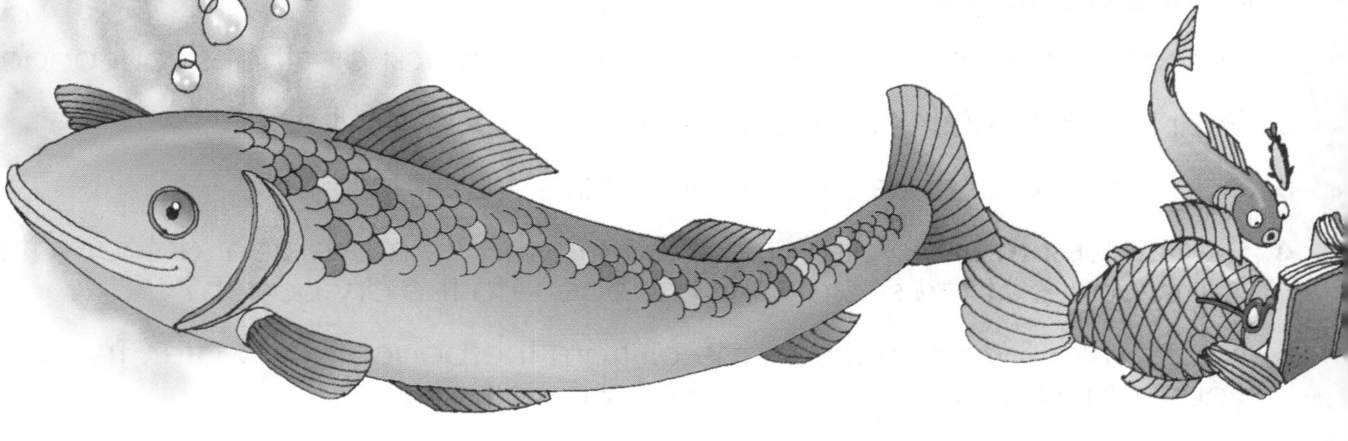

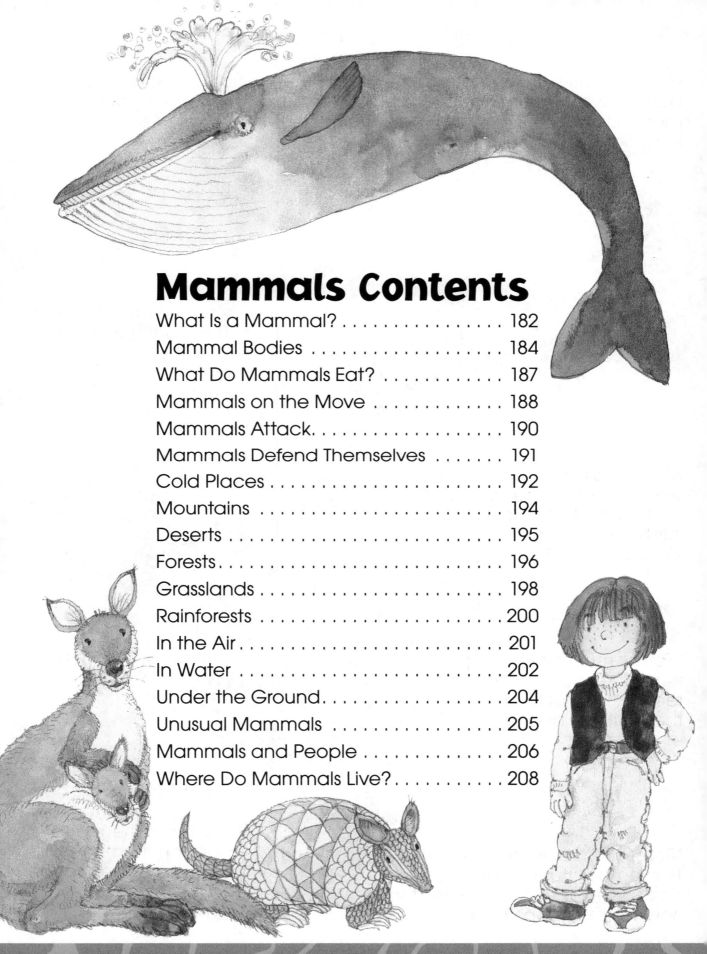

Mammals Contents

What Is a Mammal? 182

Mammal Bodies 184

What Do Mammals Eat? 187

Mammals on the Move 188

Mammals Attack. 190

Mammals Defend Themselves 191

Cold Places 192

Mountains 194

Deserts 195

Forests. 196

Grasslands 198

Rainforests 200

In the Air 201

In Water 202

Under the Ground. 204

Unusual Mammals 205

Mammals and People 206

Where Do Mammals Live? 208

What Is a Mammal?

How are you like a zebra and a whale? You don't eat grass as a zebra does or live in the ocean with the whales. Zebras and whales are mammals. People are mammals, too. All mammals are alike in five important ways.

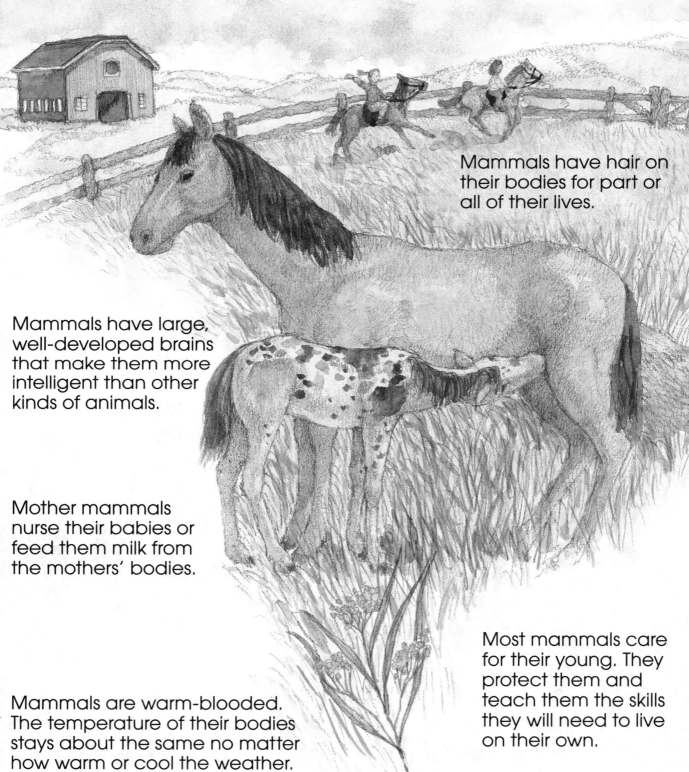

Mammals have hair on their bodies for part or all of their lives.

Mammals have large, well-developed brains that make them more intelligent than other kinds of animals.

Mother mammals nurse their babies or feed them milk from the mothers' bodies.

Most mammals care for their young. They protect them and teach them the skills they will need to live on their own.

Mammals are warm-blooded. The temperature of their bodies stays about the same no matter how warm or cool the weather.

We're All Mammals

Mammals come in different sizes and shapes. Write the names of the mammals after their descriptions. Then find the names in the puzzle.

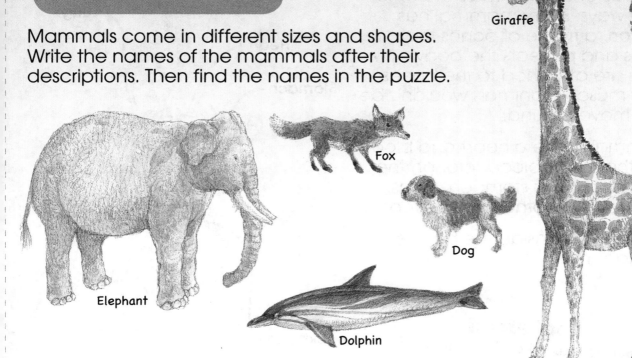

Giraffe
Bat
Fox
Dog
Elephant
Dolphin

1. I live in the ocean.

_____

2. You may think I'm a bird, but I'm not.

_____

3. I am a family pet.

_____

4. I am the tallest animal on Earth.

_____

5. I belong to the dog family, but I'm not a dog.

_____

6. I am the heaviest land animal.

_____

elephant		bat
fox		giraffe
dolphin		dog

W	D	O	G	E	B	Q	A
X	X	T	D	U	G	L	S
C	M	G	O	M	I	R	B
V	N	D	L	J	R	H	A
E	L	E	P	H	A	N	T
Q	G	O	H	Z	F	Y	A
H	I	L	I	B	F	O	I
N	C	Y	N	Z	E	B	X

Mammal Bodies

The bodies of all mammals are alike in some ways. Every mammal has a **skeleton**, a frame of bones that supports and protects the body. Muscles are attached to the bones. Without muscles, animals wouldn't be able to move around.

All mammals have a heart and blood vessels that carry blood through the body. They have a stomach, lungs, brain, and many other organs, too.

Let's take a look inside the bodies of some mammals.

Cool Word

A **species** (spee-sheez) is a group of animals that are very closely related. For example, humans are one species. Spider monkeys are another. There are over 200 species of monkeys, but only one species of humans.

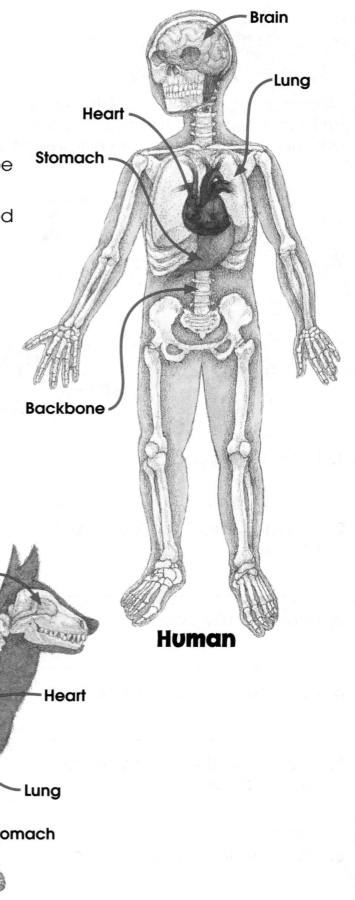

Brain

Lung

Heart

Stomach

Backbone

Human

Brain

Backbone

Heart

Lung

Stomach

Dog

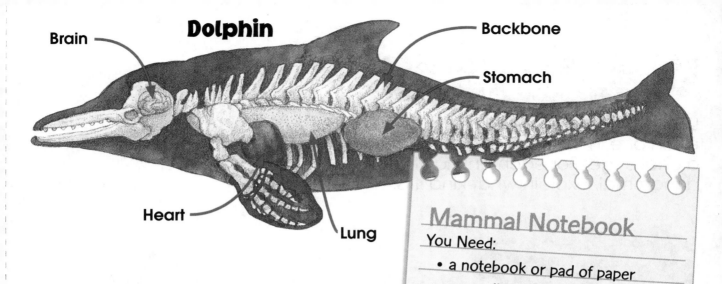

Dolphin

Brain

Backbone

Stomach

Heart

Lung

Mammal Notebook

You Need:

- a notebook or pad of paper
- a pencil
- binoculars (optional)

Go on a mammal hunt. Look for mammals in your neighborhood or at a nearby park. Draw pictures or write descriptions of some of the interesting mammals you see. Look for signs of mammals, such as tracks in mud or sand and fur caught on bushes, too.

Mammals: True or False?

Write **true** or **false** after each sentence.

1. All mammals are warm-blooded. _____

2. All mammals have tails. _____

3. All mammals have many bones in their bodies. _____

4. All mammals have four legs. _____

5. All mammals have flippers. _____

6. All mother mammals nurse their babies. _____

7. All mammals have backbones. _____

8. All mammals have lungs and stomachs. _____

Which Ones Are Mammals?

Look at the animals. Write the name of each one in the correct column. Here's a challenge: For each animal that is not a mammal, explain what kind it is.

Sea Lion

Brown Bear

Hamster

Mule Deer

Python

Llama

Green Iguana

Monarch Butterfly

Mammal	Not a Mammal/Kind of Animal

What Do Mammals Eat?

Most mammals eat plants. Plant-eating mammals, such as cows, have strong grinding teeth. Some animals eat meat only. Most animals that eat flesh must hunt for prey. They have sharp pointed teeth to catch and tear their food. Bears and skunks have teeth that grind and teeth that tear. They can eat both flesh and plants.

Mammals that hunt have good eyesight. Some see especially well at night. Their eyes are close together at the front of their heads. Hunted mammals, which usually eat plants, have widely spaced eyes.

Cool Words

Herbivores are animals that eat plants.
Carnivores are animals that eat flesh.
Omnivores are animals that eat plants and flesh.

What do you think animals that eat insects are called?

Hunters and Hunted

List each animal in the correct column.

Fox

Cat

Mouse

Squirrel

Rabbit

Wolf

Hunters

_____
_____
_____

Hunted

_____
_____
_____

Awesome!

It's not hard to guess what anteaters eat, but do you know how they do it? They use their long, sticky tongues to lick up ants. Then they swallow the ants whole.

Mammals on the Move

You can find mammals in trees, under the ground, and in the air and water. But most mammals live on the ground.

Most mammals have four legs for walking, trotting, and galloping. Humans and gorillas have broad, flat feet that help them stand upright and run and walk on two legs.

Awesome!
Flying squirrels can't really fly. They glide.

Some mammals—rabbits and kangaroos are two examples—use their strong back legs to hop. Kangaroos' long, thick tails help them balance.

Many mammals that live in trees, such as monkeys, use their tails almost like extra legs or arms. Monkeys' hands, which have thumbs and fingers, help them grasp and swing, too.

Mammals that live in water have flippers instead of arms. Whales, dolphins, and other water mammals don't have legs at all.

Bats, the only mammals that fly, have wings instead of hands and arms.

Some small mammals, such as gophers and moles, spend most of their lives underground. Moles' front legs face outward, which helps them "swim" through the soil.

Write the number of the word that
describes the way each animal moves.

1. walks
2. swings
3. hops
4. gallops
5. flies
6. digs

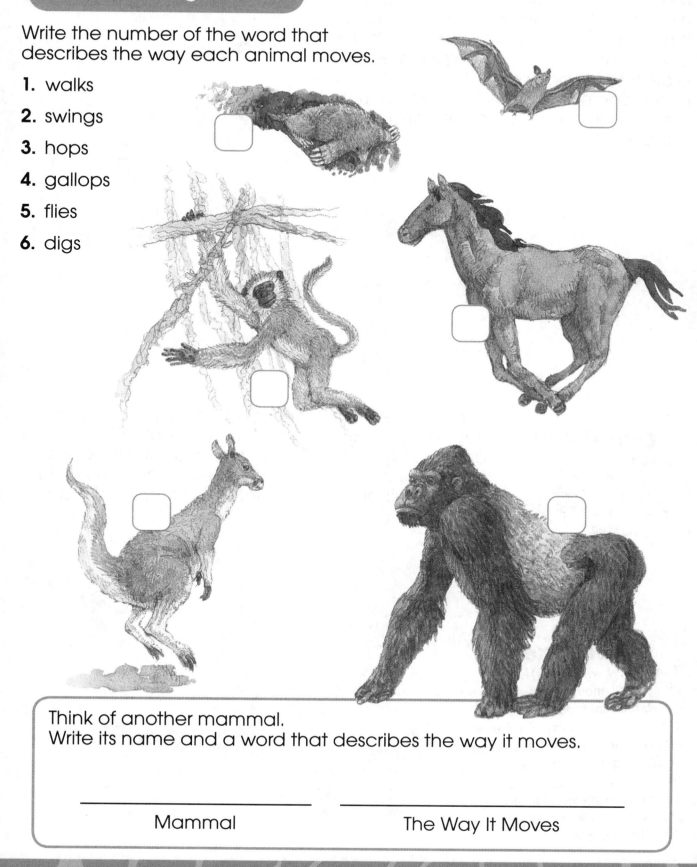

Think of another mammal.
Write its name and a word that describes the way it moves.

_____   _____
          Mammal   The Way It Moves

Mammals Attack

Most mammal hunters work alone. They hide and wait to jump out at their prey as it passes by. A male mountain lion hides at a water hole or trail waiting for prey. When a deer or elk passes by, the lion charges—often leaping as far as twenty feet. The lion uses its paw to snag the prey and kills it in just a few seconds.

Cool Words

Predators are animals that hunt other animals for food. **Prey** are animals that are hunted.

Some hunters work together in groups. Wolves are the best example. A wolf by itself couldn't catch an animal larger than a deer, but a group of wolves take turns chasing prey until they wear it out. In this way, a wolf pack can catch a 1,000-pound moose.

Awesome!

The shrew, which is the size of a small mouse, has to eat its weight in food every day. This tiny but fierce fighter is almost blind. It uses its sense of smell and its whiskers to track prey—usually insects, worms, and mice. The shrew's prey can be much bigger than the shrew!

Mammals Defend Themselves

Many mammals that are hunted find safety in groups. Muskoxen and bison form a circle around their calves to protect them. They face outward and crush predators with their hoofs.

Cool Words

Bison (bye-sun) Most people call this animal a buffalo. But the bison has a bigger head and neck than buffaloes do. It also has humped shoulders and 14 pair of ribs, rather than the 13 that buffaloes have.

Camouflage (kam-uh-flahzh) is colors and markings that help animals blend with their surroundings.

Other animals rely on speed or camouflage. In summer, the snowshoe hare is brown, so the animal is well camouflaged in the forest. As winter comes, the hare sheds its coat and grows white fur.

Skunks defend themselves by lifting their tails and spraying stinky, stinging liquid into their enemies' faces.

Some animals, such as the tiny meadow vole, don't have any special defenses. They just have lots of babies to replace the ones that are eaten.

A Sharp Defense

Use the code to fill in the letters and learn about another mammal defense.

1 = S	2 = E	3 = F	4 = U	5 = H	6 = T	7 = A	8 = P
9 = Q	10 = C	11 = I	12 = O	13 = N	14 = H	15 = R	16 = L

12 4 10 5 !   1 5 7 15 8 ,   1 6 11 3 3

9 4 11 16 16 1   8 15 12 6 2 10 6

8 12 15 10 4 8 11 13 2 1 .

Cold Places

Some mammals live in the Arctic where winters are long and dark. This far north, ice storms, blizzards, and temperatures way below zero are routine. How do mammals survive?

Polar bears have thick fur and layers of fat that keep them warm, even as they paddle through icy water with their strong front paws.

Walruses also have lots of fat, as well as tough, waterproof skin. Walruses have tusks, which they use to climb onto the ice and to fight. They use their strong, paddle-shaped front and back flippers to swim.

Cold Code

Cross off the letters v, x, and y to learn one reason walruses were important to the Inuit long ago and are still important to some Inuit today. Write the sentence on the lines.

xvyylxxnvyuxvivytyyvxyyxyx xymvxavvdyyexvy

xvxwvyaxvlxxryyuvysvxy yyfxvayxtvyv yxixxnvyvtxvoxxv

vyoxxiyvlxvv yvytxyovvx vyxbxxuyxrvvnyyy xyivvnyxx

yyxlvxvayymvypxxsvxv xyayyynxvydvxv

vvvhyxveyyaxvtyxv vxhyvvoxxvuyvsxvexysxvyy.

_____

_____

Some mammals travel thousands of miles each year to find food or warmer weather. Many kinds of whales migrate to warm waters where they give birth. In summer, they travel to cold waters to feed.

Caribou are a kind of deer that live in far northern North America. They live in Europe and Asia, too, where they're called reindeer. At the end of each summer, herds of caribou travel south. They go to evergreen forests where they can find food. In spring, the herds return to their northern homes.

Awesome!

When caribou and deer migrate south, so do wolves that hunt them. The wolves need to stay close to their food.

Match the Mammals

Here are some mammals you've met on the last few pages. Draw lines to match them to their descriptions.

Watch out when I do this!

I'm tiny but tough.

I'm not always this color.

I'm a long distance traveler.

I'm not afraid of a wolf, if it's by itself.

Mountains

High in the mountains the air is cold and hard to breathe, so mammals need warm fur and strong lungs. Sheep and goats that live in mountains have hoofs with sharp edges and rubbery bottoms to help them jump from ledge to ledge without slipping.

Some mountain mammals, the marmot is one, get fat during the summer and fall and hibernate, or sleep, during the winter. Hibernating mammals stay warm and don't need to eat very much.

Mountain & Arctic Mammals Puzzle

Use the clues to fill in the puzzle.

	hoofs	
walrus	front	polar bear
fat	rubbery	fur
skin	hibernate	zero

Across

3. Layers of _____ help keep some mammals warm.

5. The white bear of the frozen Arctic is called the _____.

7. Walrus _____ is tough and waterproof.

9. The mountain goats' hoofs are _____ on the bottom.

10. The polar bear uses its _____ legs to pull itself through the water.

Down

1. A mammal with tusks that is related to seals is the _____.

2. Thick _____ keeps some mammals warm.

4. Mountain sheep and goats have sharp _____.

6. Some mammals sleep all winter, or _____.

8. In the Arctic, temperatures below _____ are not unusual.

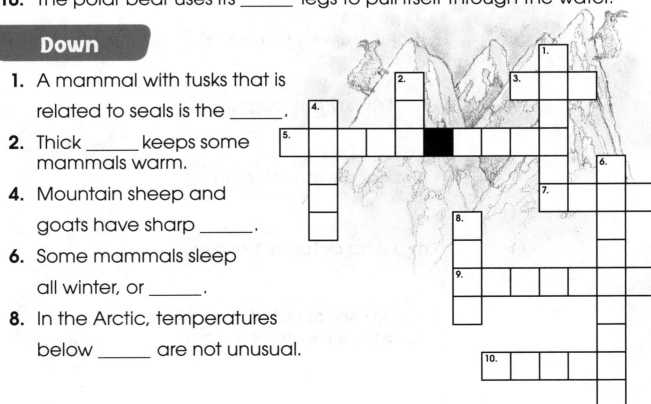

Deserts

Deserts are the world's driest places. Days may be boiling hot and nights freezing cold. Some deserts are cold all the time. How do the mammals that live in these places cope?

Many desert animals are small. In the deserts of North America, kangaroo rats burrow into the ground. They get all the water they need from the seeds they eat. Larger desert animals, such as coyotes, hide under rocks and bushes when the sun is hot. In the Sahara Desert in North Africa, mammals hide from the sun during the day and come out in the evening to search for food.

Mammals at the Water Hole

Help the fennec fox and the dromedary camel get to the water hole.

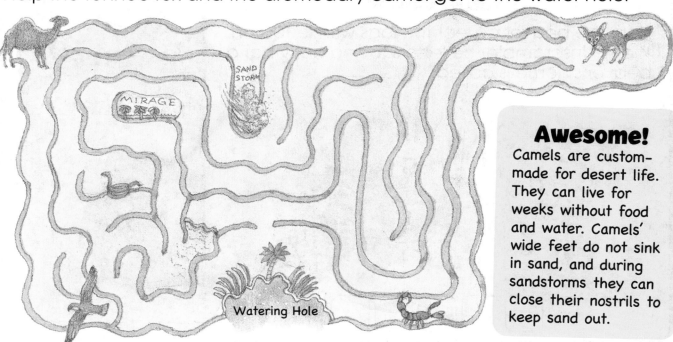

Watering Hole

Awesome!

Camels are custom-made for desert life. They can live for weeks without food and water. Camels' wide feet do not sink in sand, and during sandstorms they can close their nostrils to keep sand out.

Forests

Forests around the world are homes to many mammals—large and small. Quite a few mammals, including otters, beavers, rabbits, deer, and bears, find food and places to live in the forests of North America.

How many animals do you see in the picture?

Log Jam

Help the beaver collect the logs with letters on them. Unscramble the letters to find out what a beaver's home is called.

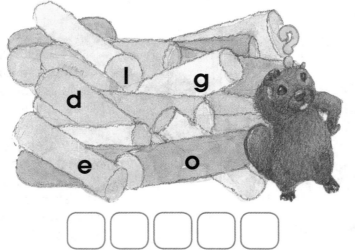

[ ] [ ] [ ] [ ] [ ]

Making Tracks

You can identify mammals by their tracks. Beavers have webbed hind feet, and deer tracks look like upside-down hearts. Raccoon tracks look almost like human footprints. Look for tracks in the dirt and mud of forests. Match each type of tracks to the mammal that made it.

Raccoon   Beaver   Deer   Rabbit

Grasslands

Many mammals make their homes in grasslands, wide-open spaces dotted with bushes and trees. Africa has some of the most interesting grassland animals. Giraffes, zebras, lions, and elephants live in the open country of Africa.

Prairie dogs and bison live in North American grasslands. Kangaroos live in the grasslands of Australia.

Stripes in the Grass

Camouflage helps many grassland mammals hide. Circle the mammals in the African grassland. How many can you find?

I'm Lost!

North American Grasslands

Below are some other grassland animals. But they've forgotten where they live! Draw lines to put them in the African grassland or the North American grassland.

Hippopotamus

Jack Rabbit

Deer

African Grasslands

Awesome!
Cheetahs are great sprinters. They can run 65 miles an hour for short distances. That's as fast as the speed limit on many highways.

Aardvark

Gnu

Coyote

Grasslands

Rainforests

Rainforests, or jungles, in South America are very hot and steamy. Rain falls nearly every day. Lots of mammals live in rainforests. Some, such as sloths, spider monkeys, and howler monkeys, live in the treetops where there is sunlight and fruit to eat.

Jaguars stalk their prey on the jungle floor, but they can climb trees when they need to. Capybaras spend most of their time in rivers.

Which Mammal Am I?

Use the clues to write the name of each mammal. Then circle the names in the puzzle.

tiger	beaver
jaguar	camel
coyote	raccoon

```
J A G U A R X Y
O R A C C O O N
C T F O R P A Q
A I P Y P G S X
M G Q O W M A G
E E Q T O K L F
L R B E A V E R
```

1. I hide under bushes and rocks in the desert. Who am I?

   _____

2. I can live without food and water for weeks. Who am I?

   _____

3. My tracks look almost like footprints. Who am I?

   _____

4. My stripes help me hide in tall grasses. Who am I?

   _____

5. I stalk prey on the jungle floor and climb trees, too. Who am I?

   _____

6. My home is called a lodge. Who am I?

   _____

In the Air

Most bats are **nocturnal**, or active at night. At dusk, many kinds of bats leave the dark caves in which they live to hunt for food. If you went into a bat cave during the day, you might see thousands of bats hanging upside down—fast asleep.

Brazilian Free-Tailed Bat

Dog-Faced Fruit Bat

Little Brown Bat

Trident Leaf-Nosed Bat

Bat Chat

What do these coded sentences say?

8 = E	10 = D	11 = V	5 = I	2 = L	6 = R
7 = M	9 = B	3 = A	4 = O	1 = P	

I'm a ⬜⬜⬜⬜⬜⬜⬜ bat.
   11 3 7 1 5 6 8

I'm the only bat that lives on the ⬜⬜⬜⬜⬜

   9 2 4 4 10

of animals.

In Water

Oceans cover more than two-thirds of Earth's surface. Some mammals, including dolphins, porpoises, and whales, live their whole lives in oceans. Their streamlined bodies help them glide easily in their watery homes. They use their powerful tails to move forward and their flippers to steer and balance.

These animals breathe air through lungs as all mammals do. They come to the surface of the water to breathe out of a blowhole at the top of their head. This can cause a huge spout of water—as high as 50 feet for some whales.

Other mammals spend much, but not all, of their time in the water. These animals are more graceful in water than on land.

Awesome!

Two mammals are the world's largest animals. The blue whale, the largest animal of all, may be 100 feet long. That's longer than a tennis court! The blue whale may weigh 200 tons.

The biggest land animal, the African elephant, is about 13 feet tall and weighs about 12 tons.

How much longer is a blue whale than an elephant is tall?

_____

How much heavier is a blue whale than an African elephant?

_____

A Whale of a Puzzle

Use the clues to fill in the puzzle.

seals
steer
blowhole
water

surface
blue
walrus

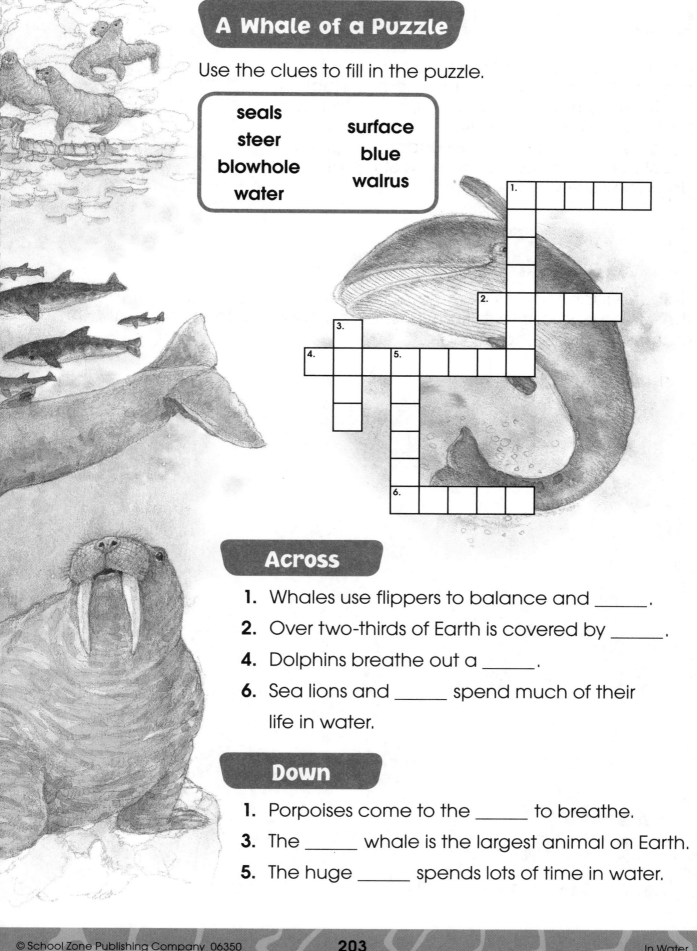

Across

1. Whales use flippers to balance and _____.
2. Over two-thirds of Earth is covered by _____.
4. Dolphins breathe out a _____.
6. Sea lions and _____ spend much of their life in water.

Down

1. Porpoises come to the _____ to breathe.
3. The _____ whale is the largest animal on Earth.
5. The huge _____ spends lots of time in water.

Under the Ground

Gophers, moles, and similar burrowing mammals make underground homes. Rabbits live in **warrens**, holes in the ground connected by tunnels. Badgers' underground nests are called **sets**. Prairie dogs live under the ground in **colonies** or **towns**. As many as 500 prairie dogs may live in one colony.

Help Them Get Home

Help the rabbit find its way through the warren to its cozy nest. Then help the prairie dog get to its fluffy nest at the center of the colony. Which mammal has the shorter path?

Awesome!
Prairie dogs kiss when they greet one another. That's how they tell their relatives from strangers.

Unusual Mammals

Australia is home to many interesting mammals. One group of mammals is called **marsupials**. Most marsupials develop in their mothers' pouches.

Kangaroos are the biggest marsupials, up to seven feet tall. About the size of a lima bean, a newborn kangaroo crawls into a pouch at the front of its mother's body. There it drinks its mother's milk and continues to grow. After a few months, the baby can leave the pouch for a while, but it continues to live in its mother's pouch for up to ten months more. Here are some other marsupials:

Awesome!

The opossum is the only marsupial that lives in North America.

Koala

Wombat

Another unusual Australian mammal is the platypus. The platypus has a hairless snout that looks like a duck's bill. Its wide, flat tail and webbed feet make it a good swimmer.

The platypus is one of the few mammals that lays eggs. Like other mammals, the babies drink their mother's milk.

Platypus

Marsupial Word Search

Circle the names of the marsupials.

wallaby	cuscus
wombat	koala
kangaroo	bandicoot

```
Q  X  N  D  R  C  K  O  C
W  F  W  O  M  B  A  T  U
A  N  M  F  J  R  N  A  S
L  D  N  D  A  H  G  P  C
L  I  K  O  A  L  A  G  U
A  C  L  Q  B  H  R  X  S
B  A  N  D  I  C  O  O  T
Y  C  Y  U  Z  E  O  L  H
```

Mammals and People

Long ago, people trained some mammals to help them. Horses, donkeys, oxen, and elephants could carry heavy loads and pull plows. Some mammals were a source of food. Cows and goats gave milk. Pigs, cattle, and sheep provided meat. Tame animals, such as cows and pigs, are called **domesticated** animals.

Sort the Mammals

The picture shows some domesticated mammals and some wild mammals. List each mammal on the chart under **Domesticated** or **Wild**.

Domesticated	Wild

Dogs and cats are mammals that have been kept as pets by people all over the world for thousands of years. People provide food and shelter for their cats and dogs. In return, their pets are loyal, playful companions.

My Dog, Pal

Do you have a pet mammal? Fill in the questionnaire. If you don't have a pet mammal, describe a friend's—or describe an imaginary pet.

Name of Pet: _____

Age: _____

Favorite Food: _____

_____

A funny thing my pet does:

_____

_____

_____

Why I like (or don't like) having a pet:

_____

_____

_____

Mammal Quiz

How well do you remember what you learned about mammals? Write **true** or **false** after each sentence. Look back at the page numbers in parentheses if you need help.

1. Mammals are warm-blooded. (Page 182)

_____

2. Some mammals have no skeleton. (Page 184)

_____

3. Mammals eat either plants or animals, but not both. (Page 187)

_____

4. Most mammals have four legs. (Page 188)

_____

5. Fur and fat help mammals live in cold places. (Page 192)

_____

6. Mammals that hibernate stay awake all winter. (Page 194)

_____

7. Many desert mammals hide from the sun during the day. (Page 195)

_____

8. No mammals lay eggs. (Page 205)

_____

Where Do Mammals Live?

Mammals live in many different kinds of home areas, or **habitats**, around the world. You can see some mammals and some of the places they live on the map.

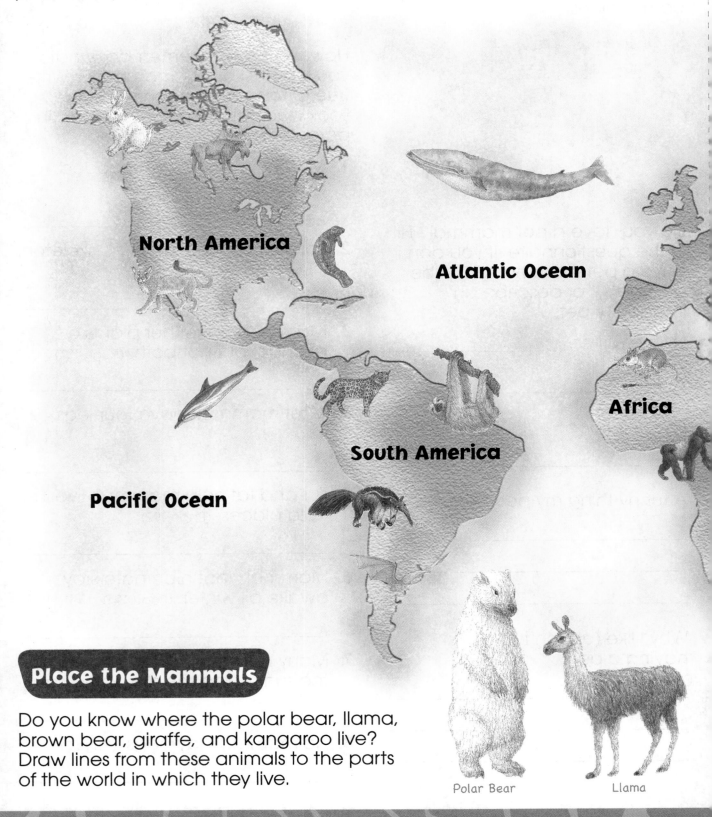

North America

Atlantic Ocean

Africa

South America

Pacific Ocean

Place the Mammals

Do you know where the polar bear, llama, brown bear, giraffe, and kangaroo live? Draw lines from these animals to the parts of the world in which they live.

Polar Bear   Llama

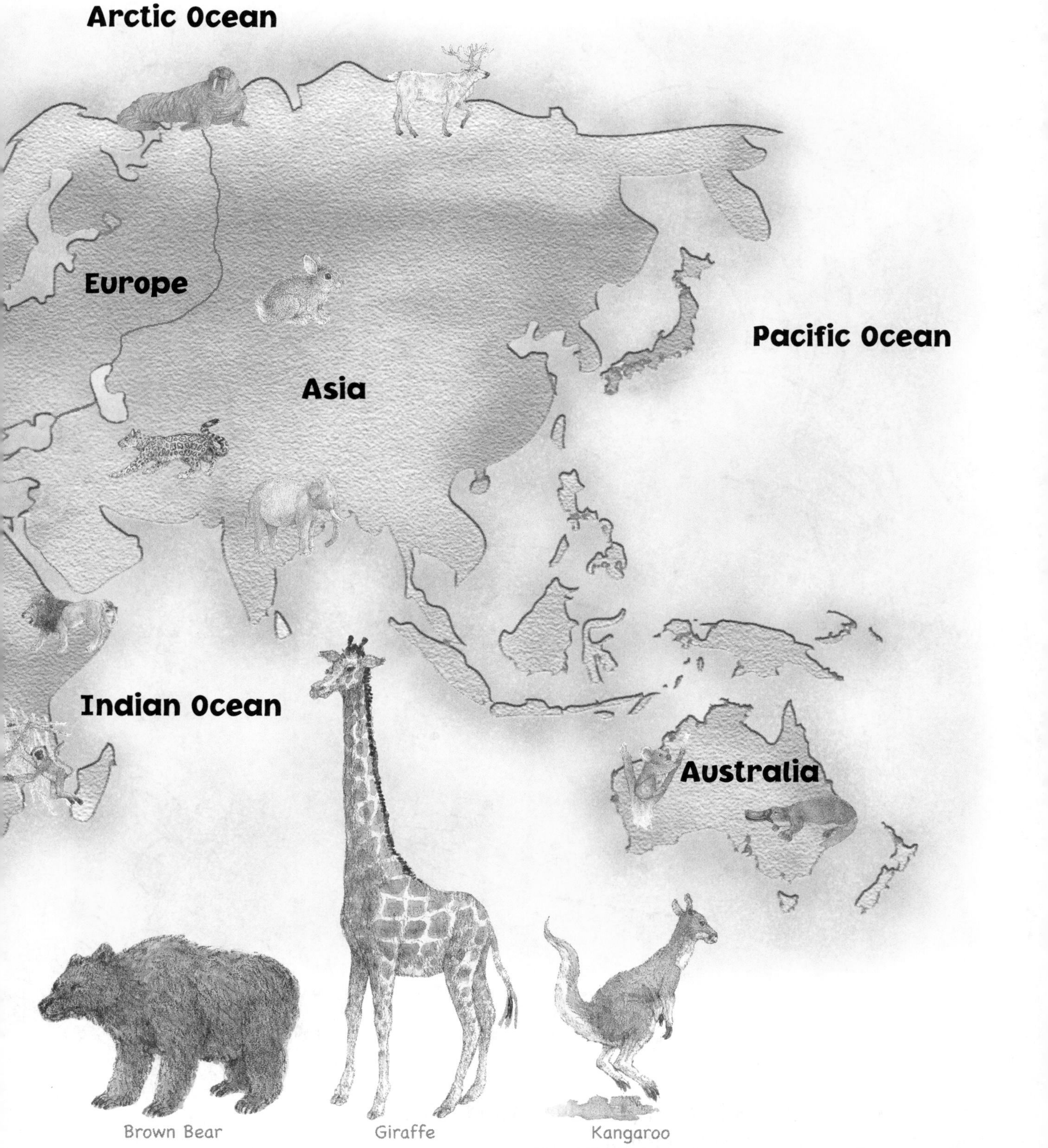

Arctic Ocean

Europe

Pacific Ocean

Asia

Indian Ocean

Australia

Brown Bear   Giraffe   Kangaroo

Rabbit

Connect the dots from **1** to **43**.
Color the picture.

Rabbits, when scared, thump the ground with
their hind feet and run underground.

Chipmunk

Connect the dots from **1** to **48**.
Color the picture.

Chipmunks are related to squirrels, but live in holes in the ground, not trees.

Deer

Connect the dots from **1** to **56**.
Color the picture.

There are many kinds of deer that live in different climates.

Toucan

Connect the dots from **1** to **52**.
Color the picture.

The toucan's bill looks big and heavy, but it does not weigh much
because it has a number of air pockets.

 Dot-to-Dots

Koala

Connect the dots from **1** to **40**.
Color the picture.

Koalas are not bears and are not related to bears.
Koalas are marsupials that have pouches they use for carrying their babies.

Jaguar

Connect the dots from **1** to **54**.
Color the picture.

Jaguars sometimes climb trees to hunt or rest.

Dot-to-Dots

Horse

Connect the dots from **1** to **59**.
Color the picture.

The hoof of a horse is just one very big toe.

Giraffe

Connect the dots from **1** to **70**.
Color the picture.

Giraffes are the tallest animals in the world.

Frog

Connect the dots from **1** to **25**.
Color the picture.

Frogs spend part of their lives as water animals and part as land animals.
A frog's life has three stages: egg, tadpole, and adult.

Elephant

Connect the dots from **1** to **65**.
Color the picture.

Elephants are the largest animals that live on land.

Dog

Connect the dots from **1** to **50**.
Color the picture.

Some of the very first pets were dogs.

Camel

Connect the dots from **1** to **71**.
Color the picture.

Camels can go for long distances across dry, hot deserts
with little food or water.

Butterfly

Connect the dots from **1** to **55**.
Color the picture.

Butterflies begin their lives as tiny eggs. After some amazing changes, they grow up to look just like their parents.

Alligator

Connect the dots from **1** to **39**.
Color the picture.

Alligators continue to grow throughout their lives.

Kangaroo

Connect the dots from **1** to **65**.
Color the picture.

Kangaroos are the largest hopping animals in the world.

Lion

Connect the dots from **1** to **47**.
Color the picture.

Lions can roar and sometimes purr. Lions live in groups called prides.

Monkey

Connect the dots from **1** to **44**.
Color the picture.

Monkeys are very playful. Monkeys sleep in trees at night.

Owl

Connect the dots from **1** to **40**.
Color the picture.

Owls sleep during the day and hunt at night.

Penguin

Connect the dots from **1** to **36**.
Color the picture.

Penguins are excellent swimmers, but they cannot fly.

Raccoon

Connect the dots from **1** to **53**.
Color the picture.

Raccoons can live in many places, even in large cities where they look for food that people have thrown away.

 Dot-to-Dots

Seal

Connect the dots from **1** to **32**.
Color the picture.

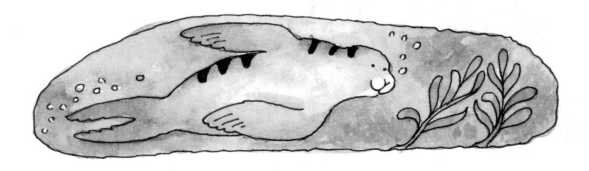

Seals are excellent swimmers, but they are very clumsy on land.

Turtle

Connect the dots from **1** to **41**.
Color the picture.

Turtles have shells on their backs for protection from other animals.

Hummingbird

Connect the dots from **1** to **43**.
Color the picture.

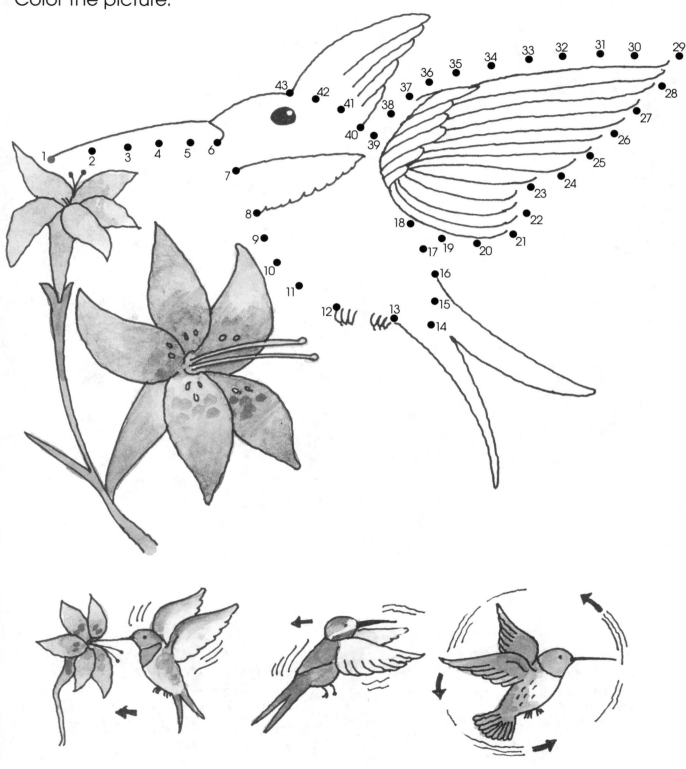

Hummingbirds can fly forward, backward, and sideways.

Zebra

Connect the dots from **1** to **54**.
Color the picture.

Zebras are wild horses that live on the open grasslands of Africa.

Panda

Connect the dots from **1** to **40**.
Color the picture.

The giant panda eats as much as 85 pounds of bamboo shoots a day!

Tiger

Connect the dots from **1** to **55**.
Color the picture.

The tiger is the largest member of the cat family.

Ostrich

Connect the dots from **1** to **40**.
Color the picture.

Ostriches cannot fly, but they can run very fast.
They are the largest living bird.

Rhinoceros

Connect the dots from **1** to **50**.
Color the picture.

Rhinos are known for the large horns above their noses. The horns continue to grow throughout the animal's life.

Gorilla

Connect the dots from **1** to **47**.
Color the picture.

Gorillas live in Africa and spend most of the day eating plants.

Mouse

Connect the dots from **1** to **86**.
Color the picture.

Mice can live almost anywhere they can find food.

Dot-to-Dots

Goat

Connect the dots from **1** to **82**.
Color the picture.

A goat less than a year old is called a kid.

Spider

Connect the dots from **1** to **64**.
Color the picture.

Spiders look scary, but out of thousands only a few are harmful to people.

Snake

Connect the dots from **1** to **58**.
Color the picture.

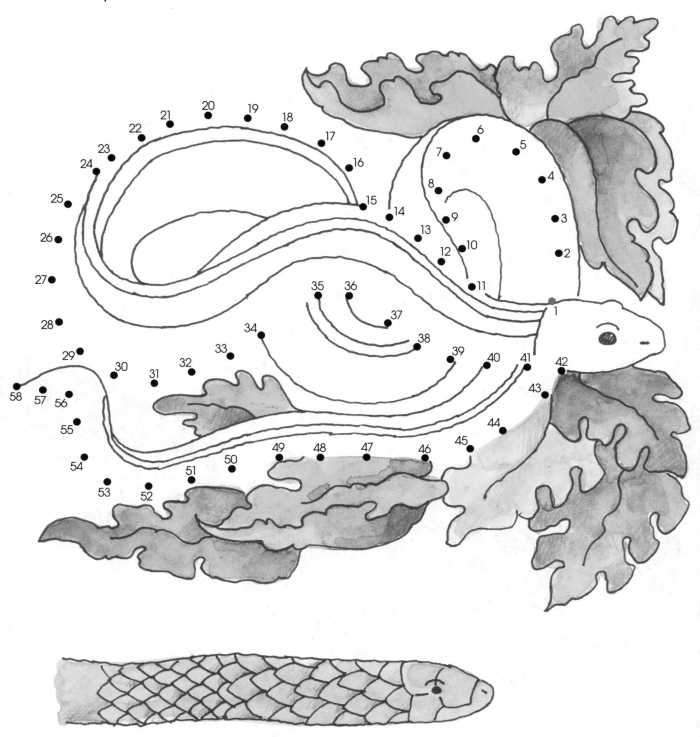

Snakes have hard scales that protect the inside of their bodies from injury.

Fox

Connect the dots from **1** to **57**.
Color the picture.

Foxes, like dogs, are members of the canine family.

Skunk

Connect the dots from **1** to **88**.
Color the picture.

Skunks are clean animals that smell fine—until they are
in danger. Then they release a very strong, bad smell.

Porcupine

Connect the dots from **1** to **41**.
Color the picture.

Porcupines protect themselves by raising the
sharp quills on their backs. They don't run!

245

Squirrel

Connect the dots from **1** to **69**.
Color the picture.

Squirrels always climb down a tree headfirst. When they jump down, they use their tails as parachutes.

Connect the dots from **1** to **66**.
Color the picture.

Pigs have snouts, which are noses. They use their snouts to
dig for vegetable roots, one of their favorite foods.

Dot-to-Dots

Sheep

Connect the dots from **1** to **41**.
Color the picture.

Every year, farmers cut a sheep's thick coat off. The wool from the coat is used to make warm clothes.

Fish

Connect the dots from **1** to **86**.
Color the picture.

Fish live almost anywhere there is water. They are an important food source for people, as well as other animals.

Dot-to-Dots

Cat

Connect the dots from **1** to **56**.
Color the picture.

The cat is a favorite pet of people around the world. Cats also provide a service by controlling mice and rodents.

250

Moose

Connect the dots from **1** to **71**.
Color the picture.

The moose is the largest member of the deer family.
The largest kind of moose lives in Alaska.

Octopus

Connect the dots from **1** to **55**.
Color the picture.

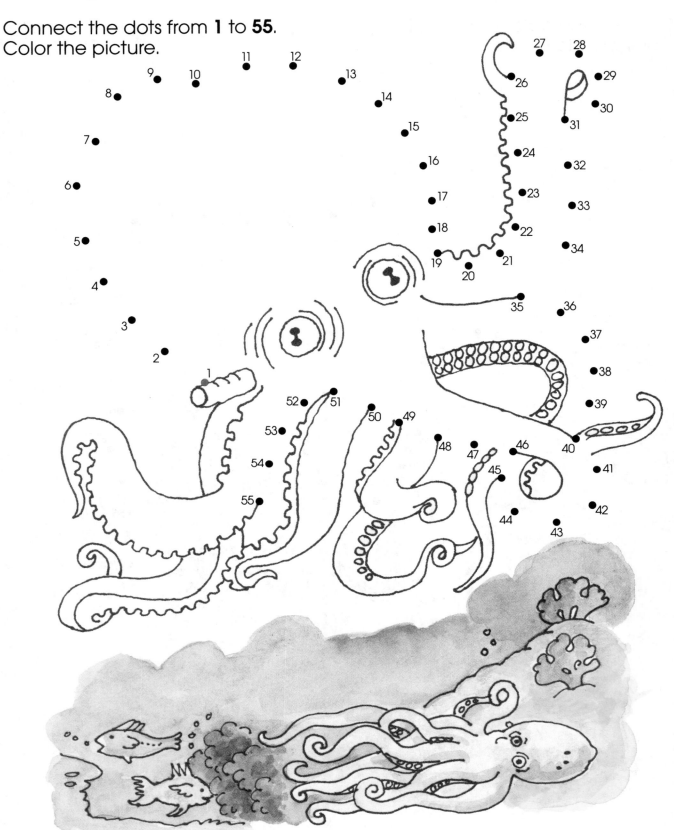

When an octopus becomes excited, it changes colors. It can also squirt liquid-like ink at animals that are chasing it.

Whale

Connect the dots from **1** to **47**.
Color the picture.

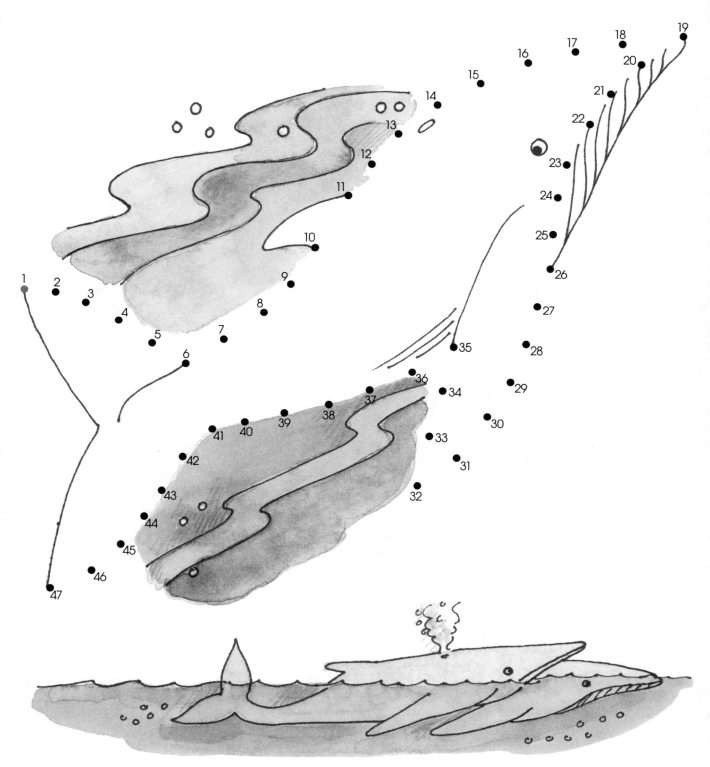

The blue whale is the largest animal on earth.
Whales are mammals, not fish.

Flamingo

Connect the dots from **1** to **59**.
Color the picture.

Flamingos live in colonies, some of which have thousands of members.
They spend their entire lives near lakes, marshes, and seas.

Duck

Connect the dots from **1** to **55**.
Color the picture.

Ducks have webbed feet that make them good swimmers and divers.
Although they are graceful in water, they waddle when they walk on land.

Chicken

Connect the dots from **1** to **59**.
Color the picture.

There are probably more chickens than any other single kind of bird.
They are raised for their eggs and meat.

Bear

Connect the dots from **1** to **61**.
Color the picture.

Bears love honey so much that they are one of the few
animals who get tooth decay.

Armadillo

Connect the dots from **1** to **66**.
Color the picture.

To protect itself, an armadillo can roll up into a ball. The hard, bony shells protect it from its enemies.

Wolf

Connect the dots from **1** to **77**.
Color the picture.

The wolf is one of the largest members of the dog family. All dogs are descended from wolves. Many people fear wolves, but wolves avoid people as much as possible.

Cow

Connect the dots from **1** to **64**.
Color the picture.

Cows are some of the most important farm animals. Cows provide milk that we drink. We also use their milk to make butter, cheese, and ice cream. Much of the meat we eat is from cows.

Bat

Connect the dots from **1** to **51**.
Color the picture.

Bats are the world's most important predators of night flying insects, such as mosquitoes and bugs that destroy crops.

Eagle

Connect the dots from **1** to **35**.
Color the picture.

There are eagles of many different sizes, from very small to very large.
They are all predators that eat other animals.

Hippopotamus

Connect the dots from **1** to **38**.
Color the picture.

Hippos are found in Africa. They spend much of their time in water.
The elephant and rhinoceros are the only land animals larger than
the hippopotamus.

Leopard

Connect the dots from **1** to **36**.
Color the picture.

Most leopards have a light tan coat with many black spots. The black leopard is so dark that the spots are hard to see. Black leopards are often called panthers.

Polar Bear

Connect the dots from **1** to **48**.
Color the picture.

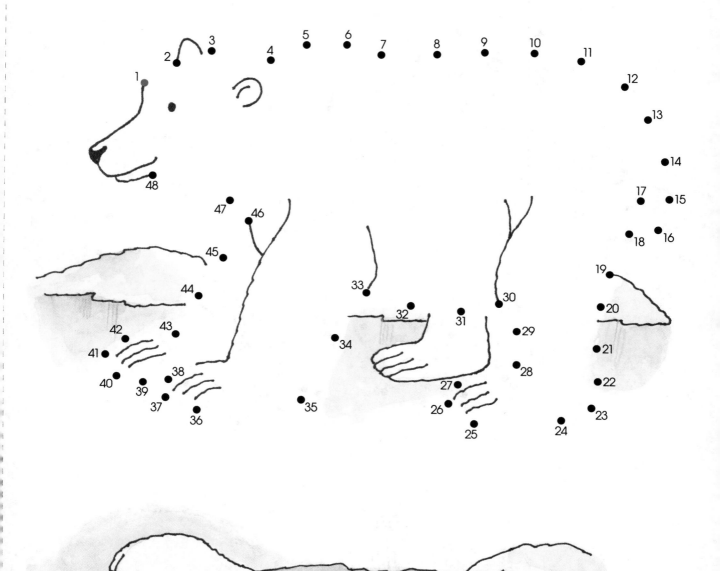

Polar bears have a keen sense of smell. They hunt seals and can sniff out seal dens that are covered by thick layers of snow and ice.

265

Walrus

Connect the dots from **1** to **46**.
Color the picture.

The walrus is classified as a kind of large seal. It is the only seal with tusks. The walrus defends itself from polar bears with its tusks.

Anteater

Connect the dots from **1** to **39**.
Color the picture.

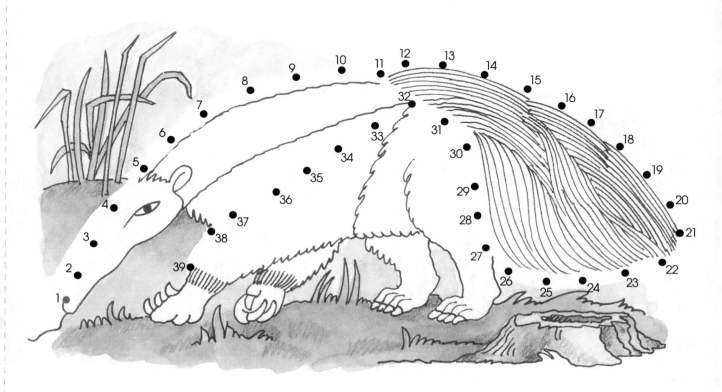

Anteaters do not have teeth. They eat ants and termites. The giant
anteater has a tongue about 2 feet long, which it uses to lick up the ants.

Platypus

Connect the dots from **1** to **47**.
Color the picture.

The platypus is a very unusual animal. It has a bill and webbed
feet like a duck and a flat tail like a beaver.

Ape

Connect the dots from **1** to **40**.
Color the picture.

Apes are closest to us in body structure and behavior. Apes rank as the most intelligent animals next to human beings.

 Dot-to-Dots

Lizard

Connect the dots from **1** to **40**.
Color the picture.

Lizards are closely related to snakes. Some lizards are legless. Others resemble snakes, but have legs.

Goose

Connect the dots from **1** to **33**.
Color the picture.

Geese are water birds, larger than ducks and smaller than swans.
Geese honk, rather than quack.

Sea Otter

Connect the dots from **1** to **45**.
Color the picture.

Sea otters are playful animals that spend most of their lives in the ocean.
They eat and sleep while floating on their backs.

As Pretty As a...Mudslide?

These similes are all mixed up! The nouns are in the wrong similes. Write the correct nouns on the lines.

1. as busy as a bug _____

2. as cold as sandpaper _____

3. as green as ice _____

4. as light as a rock _____

5. as rough as honey _____

6. as hungry as a wink _____

7. as dark as silk _____

8. as dry as a feather _____

9. as cute as a bone _____

10. as hard as a bee _____

11. as quick as a bear _____

12. as smooth as night _____

13. as white as grass _____

14. as sweet as snow _____

honey

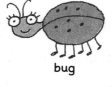

bug

rock

feather

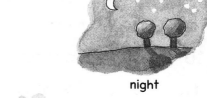

night

bee

snow

bear

wink

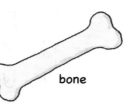

grass

silk

sandpaper

bone

ice

Fins Are to Fish...

Complete the analogies. (Analogies compare two pairs.) Then circle the words in the puzzle.

1. *Fins* are to *fish* as _____ are to *people*.

2. *Chair* is to *sit* as *bed* is to _____.

3. *Freeze* is to *cold* as _____ is to *hot*.

4. *Princess* is to *prince* as *queen* is to _____.

5. *Today* is to *present* as *yesterday* is to _____.

6. *Eight* is to *sixteen* as *nine* is to _____.

7. *Grass* is to *ground* as _____ is to *floor*.

8. *Black* is to *gray* as *red* is to _____.

9. *Scissor* is to *cut* as *hammer* is to _____.

10. *Bat* is to *baseball player* as _____ is to *writer*.

11. *Engine* is to *go* as _____ is to *stop*.

12. *Artist* is to *painting* as _____ is to *novel*.

boil	author	computer
legs	pink	brake
pound	lie	king
rug	past	eighteen

```
P O K B O I L K I C I K
B A T Q E A J N I U L N
R O S E L I E C P N J U
A L M T Q X G S Q D G E
K E I V R L E H N L B V
E G S N C N R A T T E N
Z S L C O M P U T E R P
V D O Z I D Z T V P E I
E Y P O U N D H U L F N
R U G U O T A O C J T K
B M F R X N K R V U D P
```

Do You Measure Up?

Use the clues to fill in the words.

1. It equals 1,000 grams or 2.2 pounds.

2. There are three in a yard.

3. It equals 32 ounces.

4. It's an instrument used to weigh things.

5. Use this to measure inches and feet.

6. It's a part of a whole number.

7. There are three in a tablespoon.

8. It's a fraction written with a (.).

9. Use it to measure temperature.

10. There are 12 in a foot.

11. It's about 3¼ feet.

fraction
teaspoons
kilogram
meter

thermometer
inches
feet
quart

decimal
scale
ruler

1. __ __ __ __ __ __ __ __ m

2. __ e __ __

3. __ __ a __ __

4. s __ __ __ __ __

5. __ u __ __ __

6. __ r __ __ __ __ __ __

7. __ e __ __ __ __ __ __ __

8. __ __ __ __ m __ __

9. __ __ e __ __ __ __ __ __ __ __

10. __ n __ __ __ __ __

11. __ __ t __ __ __

Solar System Riddles

Solve the riddles.
Then circle the words in the puzzle.

1. I wax and wane as I circle Earth. _____

2. I'm also called a shooting star. _____

3. I'm the biggest planet. _____

4. I'm bright and have a long tail. _____

5. I pull things toward Earth. _____

6. I'm the star around which Earth revolves. _____

7. I'm the closest planet to Earth. _____

8. We're the eight large heavenly bodies that circle the Sun. _____

9. In 2006 I was reclassified as a dwarf planet. _____

10. We've got more stars and planets than you can count. _____

11. We planets do this as we revolve around the Sun. _____

12. I'm the planet closest to the Sun. _____

Mercury

Venus

Earth

Mars

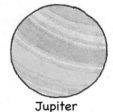
Jupiter

Saturn

Neptune

Uranus

```
P L A N E T S E L Z Y J
C Q V M E T E O R A S U
G R A V I T Y E H J K P
D V H S R Y M Z G B M I
I L E O U Q N C A F E T
N R I N C N P Z L H R E
Q O L U U D L R A S C R
G T J M T S U C X N U Q
X A C O M E T K Y D R W
V T D O K G O J P T Y S
F E X N L Y D Q K Z C P
```

Eat Right!

Use the clues to solve the puzzle.

vegetables	pasta
sugar	salt
starches	meat
fruits	fat
milk	carbohydrates

Across

5. You get energy from these in bread, rice, and potatoes.
6. This liquid is good for strong bones and teeth.
7. another word for carbohydrates
8. an oily substance that gives you energy and keeps you warm
9. This comes from ocean water. You sprinkle it on your food.
10. Spaghetti is one kind.

Down

1. It makes food sweet, but too much can cause cavities.
2. These come from plants, often taste sweet, and are good to eat every day.
3. one kind of food that has the protein you need to grow
4. These plants are grown for food. You should eat several servings a day.

Animal Habitats

Look at the animals and the places they live.
Then circle the names of the mountain and desert animals in the puzzles.
(There is no space between the words in the names.)

Mountains

Bighorn Sheep

Yak

Snow Leopard

Giant Panda

Chinchilla

Wolf Spider

V	I	T	C	O	D	N	S	H	S	E	G
A	C	Q	H	M	E	T	W	O	N	F	I
Q	B	U	I	F	I	N	O	E	O	L	A
C	D	Y	N	U	R	Y	L	Z	W	C	N
M	H	I	C	C	H	I	F	V	L	N	T
B	I	G	H	O	R	N	S	H	E	E	P
H	Q	O	I	U	S	D	P	R	O	X	A
Z	G	Y	L	N	T	B	I	C	P	E	N
N	X	Y	L	O	M	E	D	L	A	N	D
P	V	T	A	O	K	G	E	J	R	Y	A
W	E	L	B	K	P	I	R	E	D	A	C

Desert

Dromedary

Dingo

Gila Monster

Sidewinder

Elf Owl

Cactus Wren

```
G S I D E W I N D E R Q
H I D R O M E D A R Y H
B U L F I N G E T J A V
D M H A R Y T S G B B T
D L A O M I B C A F T D
N I E L F O W L X O U Y
Q O N U K D N R G S J L
G T J G T B T S X N W J
X M K B O E I L T D R P
V C A C T U S W R E N D
B E X M L Y V Q K Z R C
```

Colorific!

How many color words do you know?
Write the name of the color on each paint tube.

beige   indigo
turquoise   violet
peach   crimson
cream   olive
gold   charcoal
pumpkin   pink

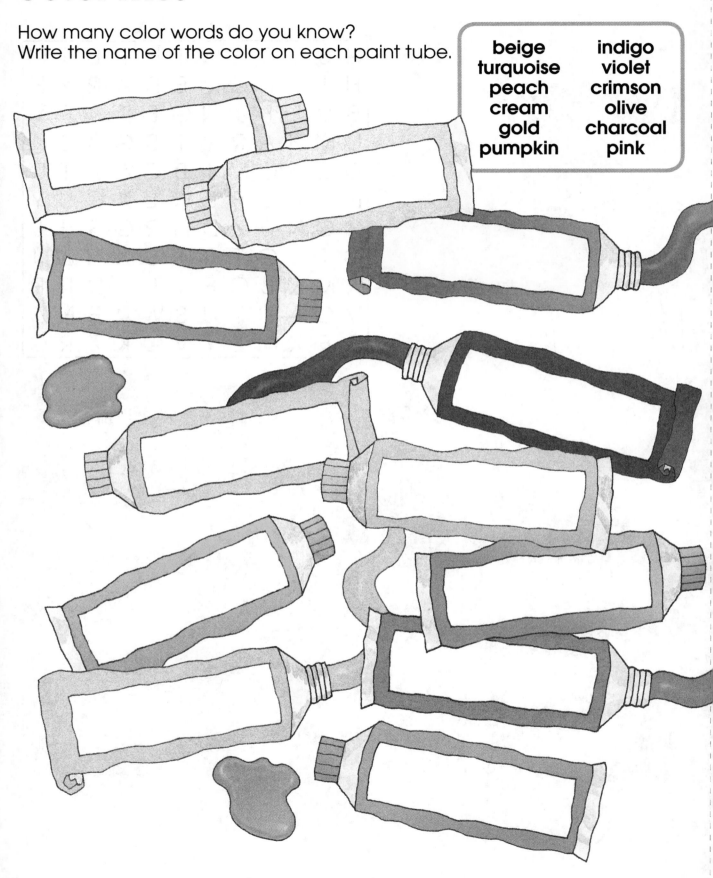

Dig This!

Some words have lost their vowels!
Fill in the missing vowels to write words about the earth.

1. The study of the earth is **glg** _____ .

2. The earth was formed **bllns** _____ of years ago.

3. Over many years, parts of the earth raise up
   to form **mntns** _____ .

4. **Lv** _____ from **vlcns** _____ cools and
   forms a layer of earth.

5. **rthqks** _____ and **wtr** _____ change
   the earth.

6. Most of the earth is covered by **cns** _____ .

7. Large **stns** _____ are called **rcks** _____ .

8. Another word for dirt or earth is **sl** _____ .

9. The rocky remains of animals and plants are **fssls** _____ .

10. A **cv** _____ is a large underground hole.

11. A **glcr** _____ is a slowly moving river of ice.

12. **Wvs** _____ wash away shores, and

    rvrs _____ eat away at mountains.

Worlds Under Water

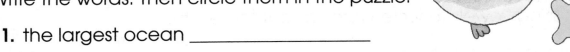

Write the words. Then circle them in the puzzle.

1. the largest ocean _____

2. These are like giant rivers in the ocean. _____

3. a large fish with rows of sharp teeth _____

4. This animal may look like a fish, but it's a mammal. _____

5. something you can taste in ocean water _____

6. a large sea mammal with tusks _____

7. an ocean animal with a soft body and eight long tentacles _____

8. the daily rise and fall of ocean water caused by the sun and moon _____

9. These form when winds move ocean water toward the shore. _____

10. tiny pieces of rock and coral _____

walrus
dolphin
sand
salt
shark
octopus
tide
currents
waves
Pacific

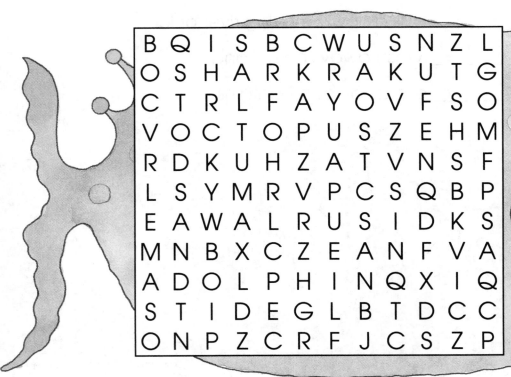

```
B Q I S B C W U S N Z L
O S H A R K R A K U T G
C T R L F A Y O V F S O
V O C T O P U S Z E H M
R D K U H Z A T V N S F
L S Y M R V P C S Q B P
E A W A L R U S I D K S
M N B X C Z E A N F V A
A D O L P H I N Q X I Q
S T I D E G L B T D C C
O N P Z C R F J C S Z P
```

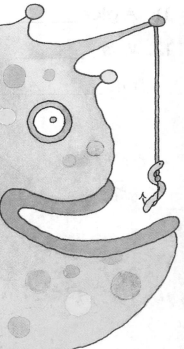

Raining Cats and...

Use the clues to solve the puzzle.

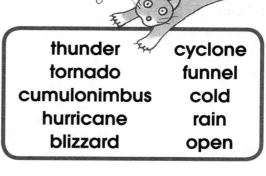

thunder	cyclone
tornado	funnel
cumulonimbus	cold
hurricane	rain
blizzard	open

Across

5. This storm, which brings strong winds and heavy rain, forms over the ocean.

6. This cloud comes with a tornado.

8. A tornado is sometimes called a _____ .

9. This storm is the most violent kind and has swirling winds.

10. A cold, windy snowstorm is a _____ .

Down

1. Hurricanes form over _____ seas.

2. Lightning comes before _____ .

3. Heavy _____ comes with thunderstorms.

4. Thunderstorms come from fluffy _____ clouds.

7. Blizzards happen when the weather is very _____ .

Them Bones!

Label the bones with words from the box.

vertebra	shin
skull	collarbone
kneecap	elbow
rib	jaw
ankle	pelvis

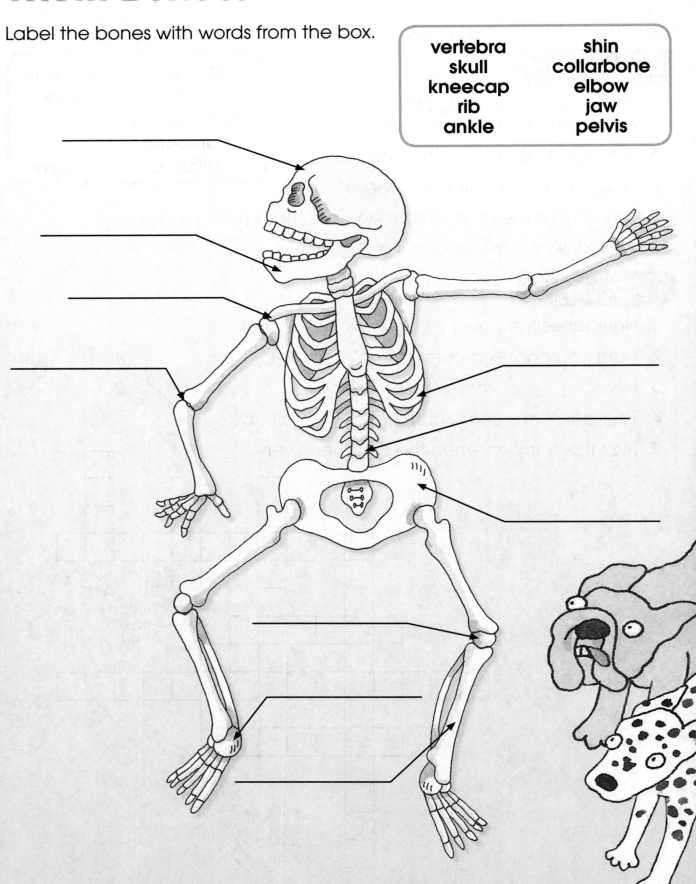

Green and Growing

Use the clues to solve the puzzle.

Across

3. We would starve without _____ from plants.
4. When we eat lettuce, we are eating these parts of the lettuce plant.
5. The _____ of plants grow underground.
7. There would be no _____ on Earth without plants.
8. Much of the _____ plants need to grow comes from rain.
10. Most plants need _____ to grow.
11. Dresses, and other _____ can be sewn from fabric made from plants.
12. We eat them and sow them to grow crops.

Down

1. This is the process by which plants make their own food from air, sun, and water.
2. When we're sick, we may take _____ made from plants.
4. Trees provide this material, which we use to build houses and furniture.
6. Plants give us oxygen, food, and _____ .
9. Plants take in carbon dioxide from the _____ .

photosynthesis
leaves
medicines
shelter
air
lumber
food

roots
life
seeds
clothes
water
sunlight

Where's My Maaaaaaaa?

Draw a line to match each mother to its baby.
Then write the name of the baby animal.

kid	colt	lamb	pup
cub	piglet	calf	fawn

sow

_____

nanny

_____

vixen

_____

lioness

_____

doe

_____

cow

A Whole Lot of Bugs!

Match the names to the animals in the maze.
Write the numbers in the boxes.
Then follow the insects—and only the insects—to get through the swamp.

1. alligator
2. bumblebee
3. butterfly
4. lizards
5. mosquito
6. spider
7. grasshopper
8. earthworm
9. firefly
10. ladybug

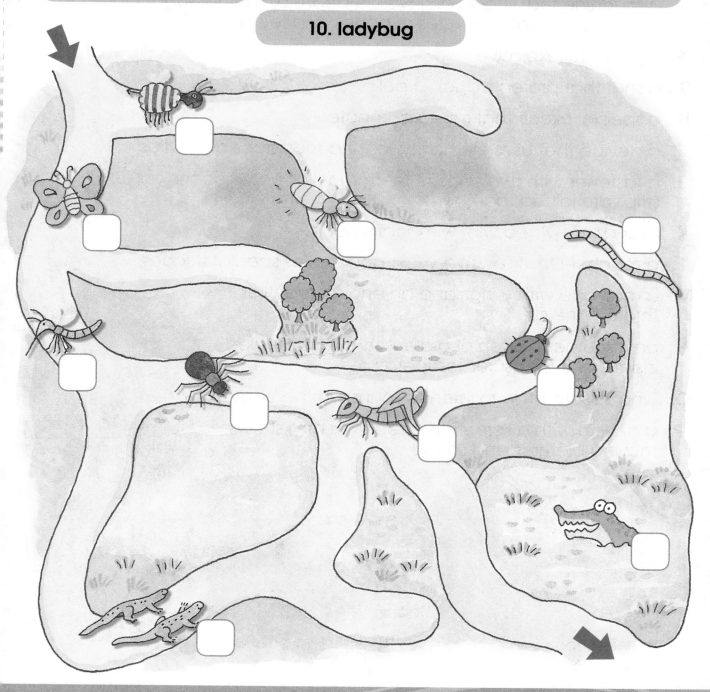

How Did They Think of That?

Match the inventions with their descriptions.
Write the letters in the boxes.

A. a space vehicle that orbits Earth, the moon, or a planet

B. a heavy gun that fires large metal balls

C. an instrument people use to view the stars and planets

D. a kind of bent pin with a guard that covers the sharp point

E. a machine that shoots an invisible beam of light through solid things to take pictures of bones and teeth

F. a powerful explosive

G. a shot that protects against polio

H. a special circuit that runs a computer

I. a device that uses electricity to send messages over wires

J. a fastener with two strips of teeth that link up when the strips are joined together

K. strands of twisted wire with sharp points

L. a machine that sews very fast and makes special stitches

M. a machine with wings and an engine that flies through the air

N. an instrument, often of glass with a liquid sealed inside, that measures temperatures

O. what doctors use to listen to sounds in the body

P. a device with a screen that receives and shows moving pictures and sound

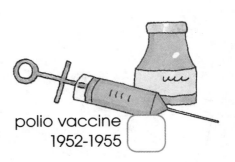

dynamite
1867

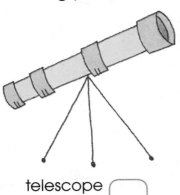

telescope
1608

television
1920s

polio vaccine
1952-1955

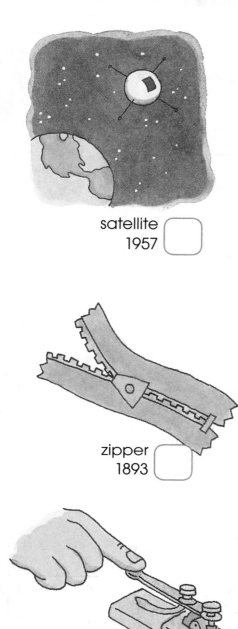

satellite
1957

safety pin
1849

cannon
about 1350

zipper
1893

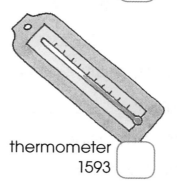

thermometer
1593

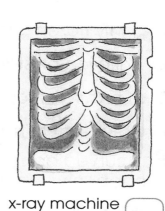

x-ray machine
1895

barbed wire
1873

sewing machine
1846

telegraph
1837

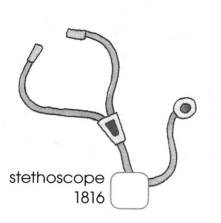

stethoscope
1816

microprocessor
1971

airplane
1903

It's a Wet, Wet World

Water covers about 70% of Earth. Write the water words after their definitions. Then circle the words in the puzzle.

1. drops of water from the air that collect overnight on cold surfaces _____

2. the white mineral in ocean water _____

3. small balls of ice that fall from the sky _____

4. a thick mist of water vapor in the air _____

5. partly frozen rain _____

6. white ice crystals, or flakes, that fall from the sky _____

7. a mixture of fog and smoke _____

8. water that falls in drops from clouds _____

9. a curved band of color that may happen when sun shines just after a shower _____

10. water drops or tiny bits of ice gathered together floating high in the sky _____

sleet	fog	rainbow	snow	rain
smog	dew	clouds	salt	hail

```
P O K N O I L K I C I H
B G V Q F A J D I U L D
C A S L E E T C E N C K
T L M T Q E W S I W L P
K E F F T X E M N R O J
E M O H B N R A K A U W
Z S G P O S M O G I D T
R H I Z I D N T V N S R
E A P S A L T O U B F D
C I I Z O T A O W O T I
B L F N X N K R V W D Q
```

Adding Up the Facts

Read each question. Circle the animal that you think is the answer. Then solve the problem. The sum gives the correct answer.

1. What mammal can eat 250 pounds of plants a day?
giraffe	214
elephant	314
leaf-cutter ant	304

$$\begin{array}{r} 246 \\ +68 \\ \hline \end{array}$$

2. What animal can lay 400 eggs at a time?
sea turtle	765
ostrich	745
sea horse	845

$$\begin{array}{r} 478 \\ +367 \\ \hline \end{array}$$

3. The world's fastest animal can travel 220 miles per hour. What is it?
peregrine falcon	777
bald eagle	677
cheetah	667

$$\begin{array}{r} 179 \\ +598 \\ \hline \end{array}$$

4. The world's largest animal can weigh 174 tons and be 110 feet long. What is it?
gray whale	1,054
blue whale	2,064
killer whale	2,054

$$\begin{array}{r} 1,456 \\ +608 \\ \hline \end{array}$$

5. What fish can swim 68 miles per hour?
blue shark	5,298
swordfish	6,208
sailfish	6,308

$$\begin{array}{r} 2,769 \\ +3,539 \\ \hline \end{array}$$

6. What animal can visit a flower 2,000 times a day for nectar?
hummingbird	12,031
butterfly	11,921
bumble bee	12,931

$$\begin{array}{r} 9,782 \\ +2,249 \\ \hline \end{array}$$

How many of your guesses were correct?

_____

Muddled Measurements

Circle the incorrect unit of measure in each sentence.
Then write the correct unit of measure on the line.

miles	feet	hours	minutes
inches	seconds	quarts	pounds

1. We counted the final ten grams before
   the Space Shuttle was launched. _____

2. The map shows that we have to travel ten
   more liters before reaching the beach house. _____

3. The cupcakes must bake in the oven
   for twenty more years. _____

4. That mouse is about three days long. _____

5. The movie was about two seconds long. _____

6. How many centigrams tall is that house? _____

7. How many minutes of milk are in one gallon? _____

8. How many meters do you weigh? _____

Measurment Match

Draw a line to match each measurement
to the tool used to find it.

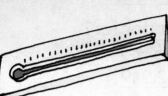

degrees

minutes

inches

It's a Fact

In 1791, a group of French
scientists proposed a new
measurement system
based on the number ten.
They thought this new
system would be easier to
use than the customary
system of inches, feet, and
yards. This new system
was the metric system.

Figuring Out Animals

Have you ever thought about the number of teeth animals have? Solve each math problem. The answer is the number of teeth for that animal.

1. An opossum has _____ teeth.

$$833 - 808$$
_____

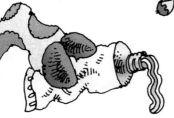

2. A giraffe has _____ teeth.

$$310 - 278$$
_____

3. A walrus has _____ teeth.

$$403 - 385$$
_____

4. A pig has _____ teeth.

$$832 - 788$$
_____

5. A kangaroo has _____ teeth.

$$670 - 638$$
_____

6. A hedgehog has _____ teeth.

$$515 - 479$$
_____

7. A lion has _____ teeth.

$$729 - 699$$
_____

8. An elephant has _____ teeth.

$$479 - 473$$
_____

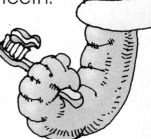

So Many Snakes!

Snakes come in a variety of colors and sizes. Read the descriptions below, then match the name of the snake to its picture. Write the correct letter in each box.

The eastern coral snake's bright stripes warn enemies to stay away.

You may not notice the colors of the timber rattlesnake, but you will notice the rattle on the end of its tail.

When threatened, the Indian cobra raises its distinctive hood.

The green tree python is hard to see among the trees of the rainforest.

> A. Green Tree Python
> B. Indian Cobra
> C. Eastern Coral Snake
> D. Timber Rattlesnake

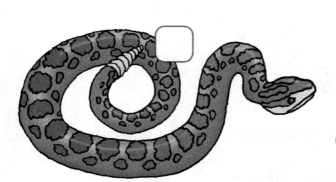

The reticulated python from southeast Asia and the anaconda from South America are the world's longest snakes. Solve the problem to find out how long they can grow!

$5 \times 6 = $ _____ feet

Dinner Time!

Small snakes eat mice, rats, fish, birds, eggs, and small reptiles. Big snakes eat large animals, such as goats or even alligators! Most snakes swallow their prey whole. Some unhinge their jaws so that their mouths can fit the food through.

Some snakes shoot poison called **venom** from their fangs into their prey. Other snakes wrap themselves around their prey and squeeze the breath out of it.

These sentences are false.
Rewrite each sentence to make it true.

It's a Fact!
Snakes have a very good sense of smell. A snake's tongue flicks in and out, bringing smells into a special organ in its mouth.

1. Small snakes eat large animals.

   _____

2. Snakes use their tongues to shoot venom.

   _____

3. Snakes use their noses to smell.

   _____

4. Some snakes grind their jaws when they eat.

   _____

5. Most snakes chew their prey.

   _____

Very Handy

Your skeleton is the bony framework that gives your body its shape and protects your organs. By the time you become an adult, your skeleton will have 206 separate bones.

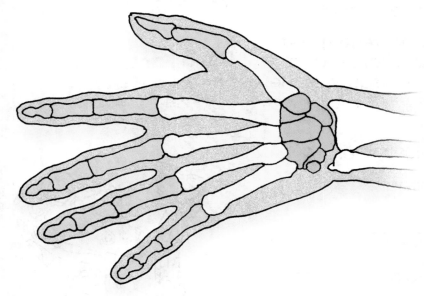

Mind Bender
These animals have body parts that act like hands. Write a verb to tell what their "hands" help them do.

_____

_____

_____

1. The **carpals** are your wrist bones.

   How many carpal bones are in one hand? _____

2. The bones in the palm of your hand are called **metacarpals**.

   How many metacarpals are there in one hand? _____

3. Your fingers and thumb bones are called **phalanges**.

   How many bones does the thumb have? _____

   How many bones does each finger have? _____

4. Suppose your metacarpals and phalanges were just one long bone.

   What would you not be able to do? _____

   _____

   _____

Made By Nature or People?

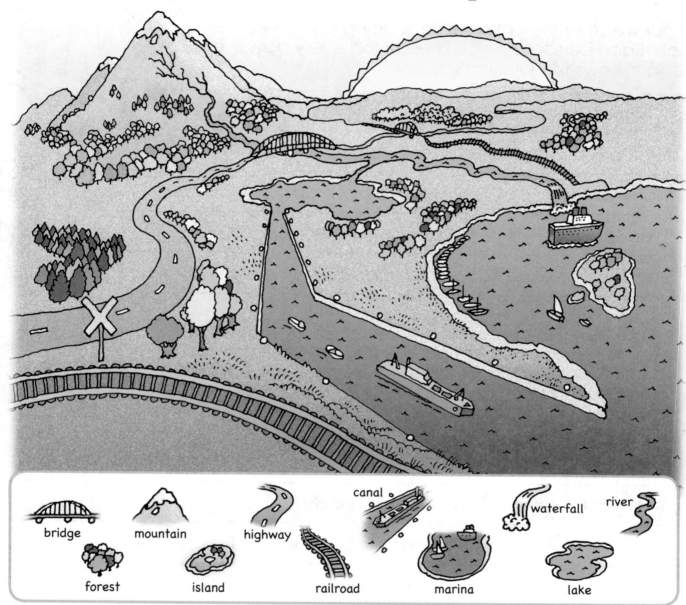

bridge mountain highway canal waterfall river

forest island railroad marina lake

On the chart, write the name of each feature listed in the map key.

Land Features		Water Features	
Natural	**Made by People**	**Natural**	**Made by People**

Who's Doing What?

Four weather experts take turns doing each weather job. Each person does a different job every day. The chart shows the jobs for Sunday.

Weather Expert	Job for Sunday
Eva Porate	Check radar and weather satellite.
Harry Cane	Create a weather map.
Wen Chill	Write a report for the newscast.
Jed Stream	Report the forecast on the nightly news.

The next day, each person's job changes by moving his or her name down the chart one row. For example, Eva's job for Monday will be to create a weather map. The last name on the chart moves up, so Jed's job on Monday will be to check the radar and weather satellite.

Fill in this chart to show what job each expert will have on Saturday. *Hint: Use a calendar.*

Weather Expert	Job for Saturday
	Check radar and weather satellite.
	Create a weather map.
	Write a report for the newscast.
	Report the forecast on the nightly news.

Mind Bender

What do you think the weather is like on other planets? Are the temperatures on Mars hotter or colder than on Earth?

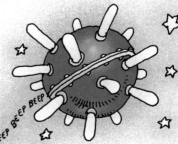

Weather Watch

What's the temperature? Look at the temperatures at Green Gardens on different days. Write the number of the word that best describes each picture.

1. hot	2. warm	3. cold	4. cool

A Clean Scene

Workers and visitors help keep Green Gardens clean. They help **recycle**, or reuse, the trash.

Sort the garbage. On the line under each piece of trash, write the bin in which it goes.

Totally True

Organize a "Litter Drive" at home or at school. To find out more, have an adult help you write to:
Defenders of Wildlife
1130 17th Street NW
Washington, DC
20036

1. _____ 2. _____

3. _____ 4. _____ 5. _____ 6. _____

Paper | Metal | Plastic | Glass

Try It!

Next time you play outdoors, pick up at least one piece of litter and put it where it can be recycled.

Subtraction Bugs

There are lots of bugs at Green Gardens.

Draw the other half of each bug. Write a subtraction problem that has the same difference as the problem on the other half. Then color in the rest of the bug.

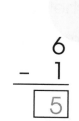

$$\begin{array}{r} 6 \\ -\ 1 \\ \hline \boxed{5} \end{array}$$

$$\begin{array}{r} 9 \\ -\ 4 \\ \hline \boxed{5} \end{array}$$

1.
$$\begin{array}{r} 17 \\ -\ 3 \\ \hline \boxed{} \end{array}$$

$$-\ \boxed{}$$

2.
$$\begin{array}{r} 18 \\ -\ 5 \\ \hline \boxed{} \end{array}$$

$$-\ \boxed{}$$

3.
$$\begin{array}{r} 9 \\ -\ 4 \\ \hline \boxed{} \end{array}$$

$$-\ \boxed{}$$

4.
$$\begin{array}{r} 18 \\ -\ 4 \\ \hline \boxed{} \end{array}$$

$$-\ \boxed{}$$

Totally True

Gardeners and fruit growers love ladybugs. Ladybugs eat aphids and scale—insects that harm plants.

6.
$$\begin{array}{r} 12 \\ -\ 9 \\ \hline \boxed{} \end{array}$$

$$-\ \boxed{}$$

5.
$$\begin{array}{r} 9 \\ -\ 7 \\ \hline \boxed{} \end{array}$$

$$-\ \boxed{}$$

What kind of insect sleeps most?

A bedbug!

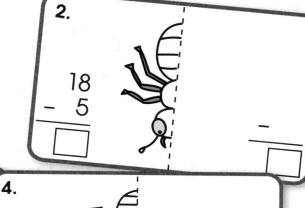

Try It!
Write all the addition facts for 10. Then write matching subtraction facts.

Subtraction

An Ento What?

Maggie knows a lot about insects. She wants to be an entomologist when she grows up.

Look at the creatures. Check the boxes next to the ones that are insects.

BUG FACTS

Wings

Head

Thorax

Abdomen

Hard Outer Covering

6 Legs

3 Body Parts

Try It!

Make a bug from materials you find around the house, such as newspapers, bottles, caps, toothpicks, and construction paper.

What is an insect after it is two days old?

Three days old!

Garden Rhymes

Words that **rhyme** end with the same sound. The word **sat** rhymes with **mat**.

Read the sentences about plants. Write the rhyming words.

1. Some plants have lots of spots.

    _____   _____

2. Some trees are slow to grow.

   _____   _____

3. Some plants have ants.

   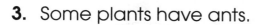 _____   _____

4. Some plants have bugs, and other plants have slugs.

   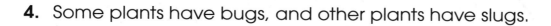 _____   _____

5. Some leaves blow in the wind as they grow.

    _____   _____

6. Some plants grow tall against a wall.

   _____   _____

Try It!

Play this game with another player.
Make two sets of letter cards.

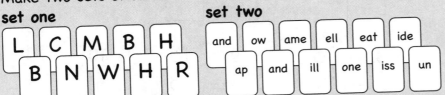

set one

L	C	M	B	H
B	N	W	H	R

set two

and	ow	ame	ell	eat	ide
ap	and	ill	one	iss	un

Put each set of cards in a jar or bowl. Take turns picking out a card from each set. If the cards make a word, write the word. The first player to make three words wins.

Totally True

Scientists believe there are more than 350,000 kinds of plants, but no one knows exactly how many kinds there are.

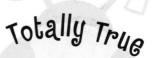

Leaf Pickup

The class is collecting fallen leaves. Subtract to finish the number wheels on the leaves.

1.

2.

3.

4.

Totally True

The sequoia trees of California are the largest living things in the world. They can grow over 300 feet high.

Try It!

Choose a number wheel. Write the addition facts to match the subtraction facts.

Write the differences.

5. 17 − 9 = ☐	**6.** 16 − 8 = ☐	**7.** 17 − 8 = ☐
8. 16 − 9 = ☐	**9.** 15 − 8 = ☐	**10.** 14 − 9 = ☐

Find the Pond

Help the frog find the path to the pond.
Start at 20 and count by 2s.

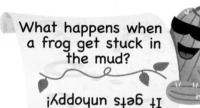

What happens when
a frog get stuck in
the mud?

It gets unhoppy!

43	32	26	22	33	36	25	22	20	28
42	40	38	36	34	28	27	24	30	29
44	45	41	35	32	30	28	26	27	28
46	48	50	56	58	60	63	65	67	27
43	42	52	54	51	62	64	59	62	74
49	62	78	91	84	67	66	68	70	72
89	95	92	95	88	86	84	82	75	74
94	96	97	93	90	81	75	80	78	76
89	92	98	91	92	91	89	83	81	79
91	88	90	95	94	96	98	100	99	94

Totally True

A frog uses its
long, sticky tongue
to capture flies and
other insects.

Try It!
Circle the tens. Then
write the tens in order
on a sheet of paper.

What's In a Book?

Kim and LaTasha want to learn more about cactuses. They choose a book about their subject. They read the contents page to find out what information is in the book.

Contents

Chapter 1
What Is a Cactus? _____ 2–7

Chapter 2
Parts of a Cactus _____ 8–14

Chapter 3
The Life of a Cactus _____ 15–24

Chapter 4
Kinds of Cactuses _____ 25–35

Chapter 5
Why Cactuses Are Important _36–47

Chapter 6
Cactuses in Trouble_____48–57

Chapter 7
Learn More about Cactuses __58–63

1. To which pages would you turn to find:

   what kind of cactus the girls saw in the greenhouse?

   _____

   the name of the sharp parts of a cactus?

   _____

   how cactuses grow?

   _____

   another book about cactuses?

   _____

   how cactuses are used in medicine?

   _____

2. What would be a good title for this book?

   _____

Totally True

Cactuses only grow a few inches a year, but they can live a long time. Some cactuses can live as long as 200 years!

Try It!

Go to the library to find books about plants that interest you. Do the books have contents pages? Read the contents pages. Which book would you most like to read? Why?

Answer Key

Page 3
Possible answers include: hot, sunny, and dry for the first picture; windy, cool, breezy, and dry for the second picture; and wet, drizzly, and soggy for the third picture.

Page 5
72°, 50°, 86°, 30°

Page 6
the north

```
B  R  E  E  Z  E  W  B  A
H  L  F  S  T  E  I  L  X
D  C  U  R  R  E  N  T  B
F  N  S  D  L  N  D  E  L
O  T  N  R  X  T  P  E  O
I  S  L  A  B  R  O  D  W
V  S  T  F  G  A  L  E  E
G  U  S  T  T  E  R  G  S
U  B  L  A  S  T  U  L  B
```

Page 10

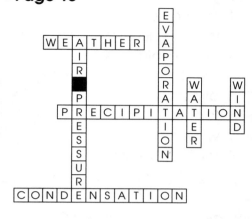

Page 11

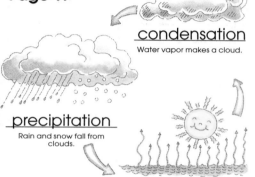

condensation
Water vapor makes a cloud.

precipitation
Rain and snow fall from clouds.

evaporation
Heat from the sun changes water into water vapor.

Page 12

Page 14
1. cumulus
2. cumulonimbus
3. cirrus
4. stratus

Page 17
The colors in the rainbow are always in the same order: red, orange, yellow, green, blue, indigo, and violet.

Page 20

Page 21

Page 22

```
W  H  I  R  L  W  I  N  D
H  L  F  X  P  I  N  L  X
D  C  Y  C  L  O  N  E  T
F  U  N  N  E  L  D  V  W
O  T  N  R  C  T  P  O  I
F  N  S  D  H  J  G  R  S
V  S  T  B  U  N  L  T  T
G  P  S  T  R  K  R  E  E
S  P  I  N  N  E  R  X  R
```

Page 23

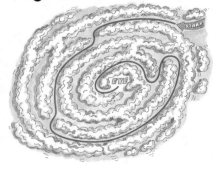

Page 24
1. tornado
2. snowstorm
3. hurricane
4. thunderstorm
5. rainbow

Page 25

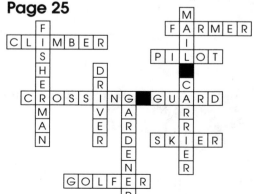

Answer Key

Page 28
1. air pressure
2. thermometer
3. cumulonimbus
4. seven
5. blizzard
6. funnel
7. waves
8. meteorologists

A WEATHER CHAMP

Page 33

Page 36
1. plants
2. embryo
3. stem
4. water
5. seeds

Page 38
coconut
watermelon
corn
1. no
2. no

Page 40
pumpkin

Page 41
hooks, barbs

Page 42

Page 43

Page 45
Drawing should include
labels that identify the part
of the plant growing up
as the shoot and the part
growing down as the root.

Page 46
1. coat
2. stem, leaves, roots
3. germinate

Page 48
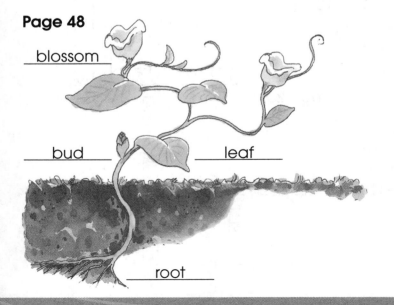
blossom
bud
leaf
root

Page 49
6, 2
4, 3
1, 5

Page 50
1. soil
2. shoot
3. root
4. energy
5. buds
6. stem

Answer Key

Page 52
1. carbon dioxide
2. from animals
3. oxygen
4. from plants

Page 53
1. tomato
2. bean
3. corn
4. lily

Page 54
1. plant C
2. 3''
3. plants A and D

Page 56
1. food
2. seeds
3. hide
4. bury
5. carry
6. drop

Page 57
1. roots
2. kernels or seeds
3. leaf or leaves

Pages 58-59
Lists should include fruits and vegetables, other articles of clothing, one product (such as maple syrup) that comes from trees, and one plant-eating animal (such as sheep).

Page 60
1. true
2. false
3. false
4. false
5. true
6. false
7. true
8. true
9. false
10. true

Page 63
abdomen, head, thorax

Page 65

Insects	Not Insects
Katydid	Millipede
Butterfly	Pill Bug
Dragonfly	Slug
	Centipede
	Earthworm
	Dog Tick
	Tarantula

Page 66
Water Striders: 5
Water Boatmen: 6
Dragonfly Nymphs: 3
Mayfly Nymphs: 4

Page 67
All the insects listed in the word box are shown in the picture.

Page 71
1. egg
2. plant
3. larva
4. caterpillar
5. skin
6. butterfly
7. pupa
8. four

Page 68

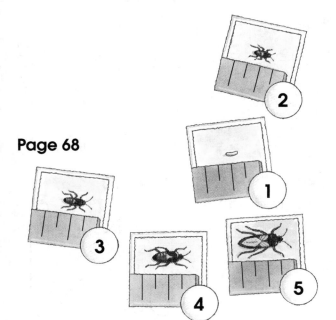

Answer Key

Page 75

10 walking sticks

Page 78
total number of insects: 50
(includes fleas on and near dog)

Page 79
1. vegetables
2. germs
3. hatch
4. honey
5. ants
6. soil

T E R M I T E

Page 81

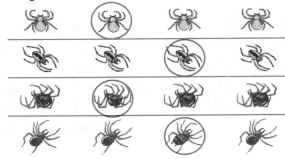

Page 83

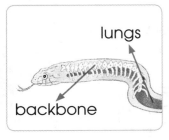

S
SPINNERETS S
L I W
K G POISON
H
INSECTS

Page 85
HELP!
SNAKES, FROGS,
AND BIRDS ARE AFTER
ME! THEY WANT TO EAT
ME FOR LUNCH!
SPIDER

Page 87
Answers will vary, but all
foods must be liquids.

Page 92
Total number of reptiles: 12
The girl is not a reptile.

Page 93

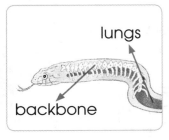

lungs

backbone

Page 94
Antarctica
Most children
will guess that
Antarctica is
too cold for
reptiles.

Page 95

Page 96

P
LUNGS
A B R
TEMPERATURE E
A C P
T K T
E B I
S O L
LAND E
S

Page 97
Gila monster

Page 98

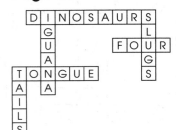

DINOSAURS
G L
U FOUR
A G
TONGUE S
A A
I
L
S

Page 99
1. Komodo dragon
2. skink
3. gecko
4. iguana
5. flying dragon

Page 100

Answer Key

Page 101
About 6 feet
About 18 feet

Page 103

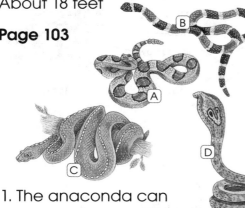

1. The anaconda can grow as long as **30** feet.
2. Most snakes **don't** take care of their babies.
3. Snakes that live in **deserts** move by sidewinding.
4. Snakes use their **tongues** to sense smells.

Page 105
35 baby sea turtles
1. land
2. water
3. land
4. water

Page 106
1,000 pounds

Page 107

Page 108

Crocodiles & Alligators
alligator

Snakes
anaconda
boa
python

Turtles & Tortoises
tortoise

Lizards
gecko
chameleon
iguana

Page 109

Page 110

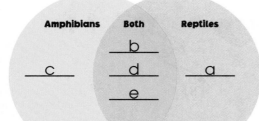

Amphibians — c

Both — b, d, e

Reptiles — a

Page 111

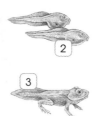

Page 112
Most children will write that salamanders hunt at night to avoid the sun.

Page 113
Grow another one!

Children should draw salamanders in each of the environments except the desert.

Answer Key

Page 114
1. 11½ inches
2. 80 feet
3. 20 feet

Page 115
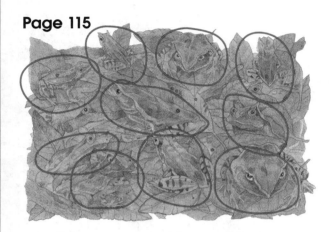

Page 117
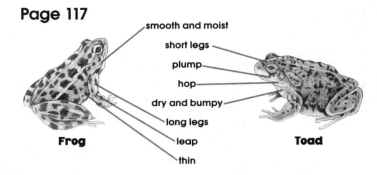

smooth and moist
short legs
plump
hop
dry and bumpy
long legs
leap
thin

Frog   **Toad**

Page 118
1. toad
2. salamander
3. frog

1. true
2. true
3. false
4. true
5. false

Pages 122-123
Ducks, owls, and penguins should be checked.

Page 125
1. warmer
2. hollow
3. food
4. rocket
5. air sacs
6. tail

feathers

Page 127
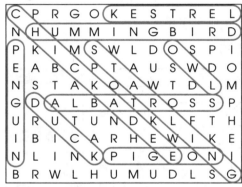

C	P	R	G	O	K	E	S	T	R	E	L
N	H	U	M	M	I	N	G	B	I	R	D
P	K	I	M	S	W	L	D	O	S	P	I
E	A	B	C	P	T	A	U	S	W	D	O
N	S	T	A	K	O	A	W	T	D	L	M
G	D	A	L	B	A	T	R	O	S	S	P
U	R	U	T	U	N	D	K	L	F	T	H
I	B	I	C	A	R	H	E	W	I	K	E
N	L	I	N	K	P	I	G	E	O	N	I
B	R	W	L	H	U	M	U	D	L	S	G

Page 129
Pelican has 27 fish including the one in its bill.

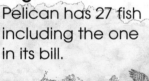

P	A	G	N	S	C	R	L	F
F	M	P	D	E	L	L	P	R
R	I	N	S	E	C	T	S	O
N	C	S	I	D	I	T	E	G
D	E	F	H	S	M	E	A	S
S	G	P	L	A	N	T	S	R

Page 130
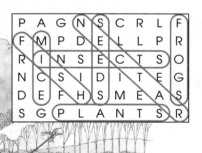

2
4
6
1
3
5

Answer Key

Page 131

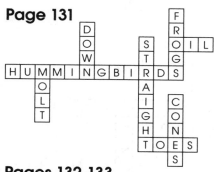

Pages 132-133

1. pigeon
2. woodpecker
3. elf owl
4. oriole
5. bluebird
6. ovenbird

Pages 134-135

48 eggs

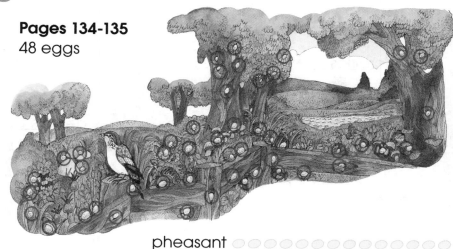

pheasant ○○○○○○○○○○○○○○○○○

Pages 136-137

C=30, F=60, G=70, L=120, N=140, R=180,
S=190, W=230, Y=250

Answer: It is getting crowded in this
nest. Watch me flap my wings
and fly out!

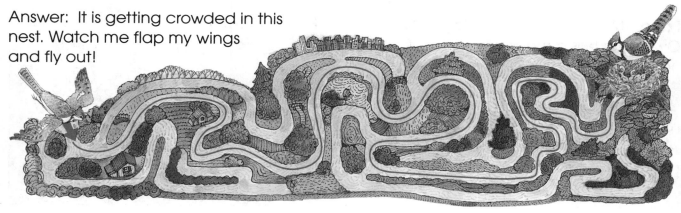

Page 139

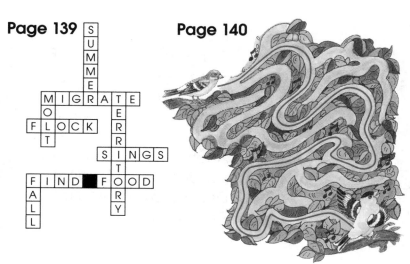

Page 140

Page 141

1. Canada Warbler
2. Sanderling
3. Phalarope
4. Bobolink
5. American White Pelican

Answer Key

Page 142

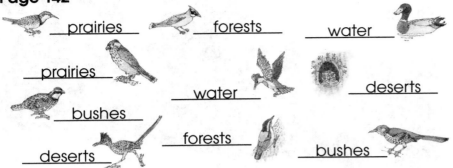

prairies   forests   water

prairies

bushes   water   deserts

deserts   forests   bushes

Page 145

1. blue jay
2. nuthatch
3. goldfinch
4. pigeon
5. cardinal
6. robin

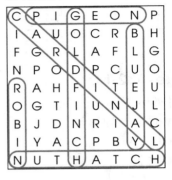

Page 147

Owl pellet has a mouse;
hawk pellet has a bird.

1. owl
2. both
3. hawk
4. owl
5. owl

Page 149

H	call	A	talon
E	incubate	J	molt
G	egg tooth	I	preen
C	flock	K	song
D	gizzard	B	clutch
F	ornithologist		

Pages 152-153

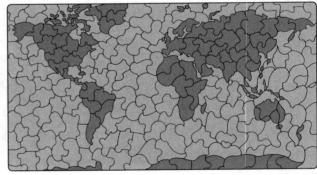

land

water

Page 155

in the ocean

1. true
2. false
3. true
4. true
5. false

Pages 156-157

Fish:

Flying Fish
Swordfish
Tuna
Skate
Cod
Anchovies
Halibut
Deep Sea
Anglerfish

Gulper Eel
Basking
Sharks
Viperfish
Hatchetfish
Lanternfish
Tripodfish
Manta Ray

Answer Key

Page 159

v e r t e b r a t e s

Page 160

Pilotfish **A** is going faster because its fins are close to its body.

Page 161

3
5
1
4
2

Page 165

Plants	Animals
Kelp	Limpets
Brown	Periwinkles
Seaweed	Starfish
Bladder	Green Crab
Wrack	Mussels
Knotted	Clingfish
Wrack	Goby
Sugar Kelp	Anemone
Sea Lettuce	Barnacles
	Sea Snails

Page 167

```
W
A
V
E   S
K E L P ■ F O R E S T S          R
            R O C K F I S E        I
      P                              D
S E A H O R S E                      A
      L                              L
      Y           R O O T S     P    T I D
      P                         O    I
      S   C O R A L ■ R E E F S L    D E S
```

Page 169

b a s k e t b a l l s

Page 171

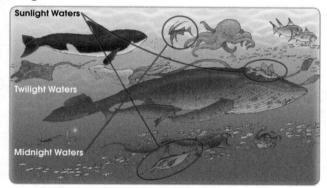

Sunlight Waters
Twilight Waters
Midnight Waters

Answers will vary.

Pages 172-173

One of several possible paths through the maze is shown.

Answer Key

Page 175
1. Beluga Whale
2. Fin Whale
3. 20 feet
4. 85 feet

Page 177

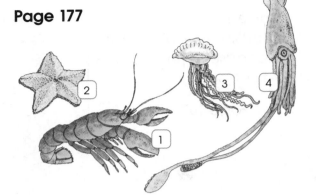

Page 178

```
A P E L I C A N W
K L D F J O S W P
I C B Q P R M S E
T S W A E M O F N
T E R N T O G K G
I A D U R R W M U
W G S I E A O Q I
A U Y F L N Q S N
K L J F U T B X S
E L P U F F I N Q
```

Page 183
1. dolphin
2. bat
3. dog
4. giraffe
5. fox
6. elephant

```
W D O G E B Q A
X X T D U G L S
C M G O M I R B
V N D L J R H A
E L E P H A N T
Q G O H Z F Y A
H I L I B F O I
N C Y N Z E B X
```

Page 185
1. true
2. false
3. true
4. false
5. false
6. true
7. true
8. true

Page 186

Mammal	Not a mammal/ Kind of Animal
Brown Bear	Monarch Butterfly/Insect
Hamster	Iguana/Reptile
Mule Deer	Python/Reptile
Sea Lion	
Llama	

Page 187
insectivores

Hunters: fox, cat, wolf
Hunted: squirrel, rabbit, mouse

Page 189

Answers will vary, but should include the name of a mammal and an action verb.

Page 191
OUCH! SHARP, STIFF QUILLS PROTECT PORCUPINES.

Page 192
Inuit made walrus fat into oil to burn in lamps and heat houses.

Page 193

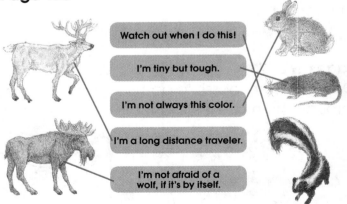

Watch out when I do this!

I'm tiny but tough.

I'm not always this color.

I'm a long distance traveler.

I'm not afraid of a wolf, if it's by itself.

Answer Key

Page 194

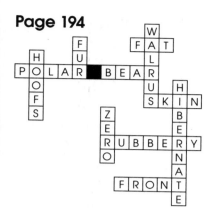

Page 195

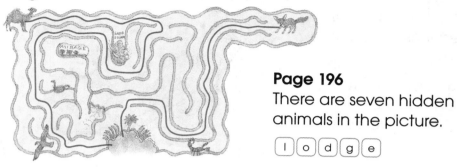

Page 196
There are seven hidden animals in the picture.

l o d g e

Page 197

Pages 198-199

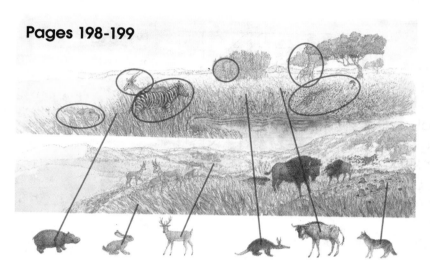

Page 200

1. coyote
2. camel
3. raccoon
4. tiger
5. jaguar
6. beaver

Page 201
vampire
blood

Page 202
87 feet
188 tons

Page 203

Page 204

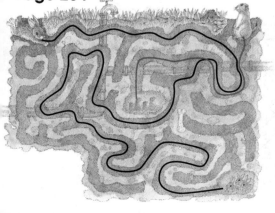

Page 205

Page 206
Domesticated:
cow
goat
horse
pig
dog
cat
sheep

Wild:
fox
rabbit
mouse
raccoon

Answer Key

Page 207
Pet questionnaire responses will vary.

1. true   2. false
3. false   4. true
5. true   6. false
7. true   8. false

Pages 208-209

Page 274
1. legs
2. lie
3. boil
4. king
5. past
6. eighteen
7. rug
8. pink
9. pound
10. computer
11. brake
12. author

Page 273
1. bee
2. ice
3. grass
4. feather
5. sandpaper
6. bear
7. night
8. bone
9. bug
10. rock
11. wink
12. silk
13. snow
14. honey

Page 275
1. k i l o g r a m
2. f e e t
3. q u a r t
4. s c a l e
5. r u l e r
6. f r a c t i o n
7. t e a s p o o n s
8. d e c i m a l
9. t h e r m o m e t e r
10. i n c h e s
11. m e t e r

Page 276
1. Moon
2. meteor
3. Jupiter
4. comet
5. gravity
6. Sun
7. Venus
8. planets
9. Pluto
10. galaxy
11. rotate
12. Mercury

Page 277

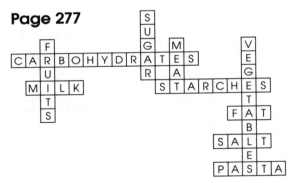

Page 278

Page 279

Page 280

Answer Key

Page 281
1. geology
2. billions
3. mountains
4. Lava; volcanoes
5. Earthquakes; water
6. oceans
7. stones; rocks
8. soil
9. fossils
10. cave
11. glacier
12. Waves; rivers

Page 282
1. Pacific
2. currents
3. shark
4. dolphin
5. salt
6. walrus
7. octopus
8. tide
9. waves
10. sand

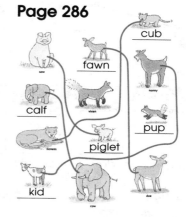

Page 283

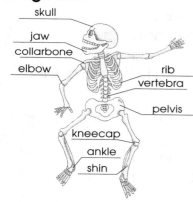

Page 284

skull
jaw
collarbone
elbow
rib
vertebra
pelvis
kneecap
ankle
shin

Page 285

LEAVES
LIFE
WATER
SUNLIGHT
CLOTHES
SEEDS
FOOD
ROOTS
PHOTOSYNTHESIS
SHELTER
LUMBER
MEDICINE
FIRE

Page 286

cub
fawn
calf
pup
piglet
kid

Page 287

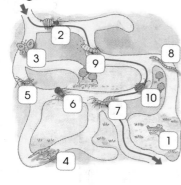

Pages 288–289
A. satellite
B. cannon
C. telescope
D. safety pin
E. X-ray machine
F. dynamite
G. polio vaccine
H. microprocessor
I. telegraph
J. zipper
K. barbed wire
L. sewing machine
M. airplane
N. thermometer
O. stethoscope
P. television

Page 290
1. dew
2. salt
3. hail
4. fog
5. sleet
6. snow
7. smog
8. rain
9. rainbow
10. clouds

Page 291
1. elephant 314
2. sea horse 845
3. peregrine falcon 777
4. blue whale 2,064
5. sailfish 6,308
6. hummingbird 12,031

Answer Key

Page 292
Circled/Correct
1. grams/seconds
2. liters/miles
3. years/minutes
4. days/inches
5. seconds/hours
6. centigrams/feet
7. minutes/quarts
8. meters/pounds

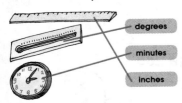
- degrees
- minutes
- inches

Page 293
1. 25
2. 32
3. 18
4. 44
5. 32
6. 36
7. 30
8. 6

Page 294

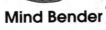

Mind Bender
5x6 = 30 feet

Page 296
1. 8
2. 5
3. 2, 3
4. bend your fingers

Mind Bender
dig, fly, swim

Page 295
Sentences may vary.
1. Big snakes eat large animals.
2. Snakes use their fangs to shoot venom.
3. Snakes use their tongues to smell.
4. Some snakes unhinge their jaws when they eat.
5. Most snakes swallow their prey whole.

Page 297

Land Features		Water Features	
Natural	Made by People	Natural	Made by People
island	highway	lake	marina
forest	railroad	river	canal
mountain	bridge	waterfall	

Page 298
1. Wen/Check radar and weather satellite.
2. Jed/Create a weather map.
3. Eva/Write a report for the newscast.
4. Harry/Report the forecast on the nightly news.

Mind Bender Temperatures on Mars are colder than on Earth.

Page 299
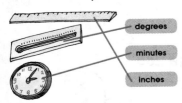

Page 300
1. plastic
2. metal
3. paper
4. glass
5. plastic
6. paper

Page 301
Subtraction problems will vary, but differences should be the same as in each item.
Example:

1. $\begin{array}{r} 17 \\ -\ 3 \\ \hline 14 \end{array}$ $\begin{array}{r} 19 \\ -\ 5 \\ \hline 14 \end{array}$
2. $\begin{array}{r} 18 \\ -\ 5 \\ \hline 13 \end{array}$ $\begin{array}{r} 20 \\ -\ 7 \\ \hline 13 \end{array}$

3. $\begin{array}{r} 9 \\ -\ 4 \\ \hline 5 \end{array}$ $\begin{array}{r} 12 \\ -\ 7 \\ \hline 5 \end{array}$
4. $\begin{array}{r} 18 \\ -\ 4 \\ \hline 14 \end{array}$ $\begin{array}{r} 16 \\ -\ 2 \\ \hline 14 \end{array}$

5. $\begin{array}{r} 12 \\ -\ 9 \\ \hline 3 \end{array}$ $\begin{array}{r} 7 \\ -\ 4 \\ \hline 3 \end{array}$
6. $\begin{array}{r} 9 \\ -\ 7 \\ \hline 2 \end{array}$ $\begin{array}{r} 13 \\ -11 \\ \hline 2 \end{array}$

Page 302

Page 303
1. lots — spots
2. grow — slow
3. plants — ants
4. bugs — slugs
5. blow — grow
6. tall — wall

Page 304
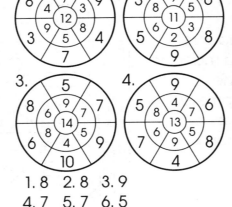

1. 8   2. 8   3. 9
4. 7   5. 7   6. 5

Page 305

43	32	26	22	33	36	25	22	20	28
42	40	38	36	34	28	27	24	30	29
44	45	41	35	32	30	28	26	27	28
46	48	50	56	58	60	63	65	67	27
43	42	52	54	51	62	64	59	62	74
49	62	78	91	84	67	66	68	70	72
89	95	92	95	88	86	84	82	75	74
94	96	97	93	90	81	75	80	78	76
89	92	98	91	92	91	89	83	81	79
91	88	90	95	94	96	98	100	99	94

Page 306
1. 25, 8, 15, 58, 36
2. Answers should include the word cactus.

Big Science 06350